BEARS
of the
WORLD

BEARS
of the
WORLD

Terry Domico

PHOTOGRAPHS BY

Terry Domico and

Mark Newman

Facts On File®

New York • Oxford

Library of Congress Cataloging-in-Publication Data

Domico, Terry.
  Bears of the world.

  Bibliography: p.
  Includes index.
  1. Bears—Popular works. 2. Mammals—Popular works. I. Title.
QL737.C27D65 1988   599.74'446   88-3881
ISBN 0-8160-1536-8

Illustration on p. 147 is used by permission
of the USDA Forest Service.

Jacket and interior design
by Beth Tondreau Design/Carol Barr

Printed in the United States

10 9 8 7 6 5 4 3

BOMC offers recordings and compact discs, cassettes
and records. For information and catalog write to
BOMR, Camp Hill, PA 17012.

To my mother,
who originally encouraged
my nature studies,
and to Robin,
with whom it is my turn.

CONTENTS

PREFACE

Throughout history humans have been influenced by the existence of the bear. To many, the bear has become a living symbol of the untouched wilderness, of clear lakes and primeval forests. To others, the bear is a spiritual force, revered and sacred, capable of healing or renewal. In our vision the bear can range from shuffling clown to demonic beast of legendary ferocity. Clearly there is something about these animals that pulls at the emotions and stimulates our interest.

I met my first bear when I was a boy of seventeen in the western American state of Idaho, where I grew up. My two younger brothers and I were on a week-long trek along Cottonwood Creek trail in the Sawtooth Mountains. We had just broken camp and were starting the day's climb toward timberline when Steve, the youngest, saw it.

"A bear!"

We froze in our tracks and followed Steve's gaze down to the creek. Thirty feet away, an animal as big as a horse with a shaggy coat of silvery brown fur lunged at a fish. He sensed our presence and stood up to face us. It was a grizzly, a North American variety of brown bear.

He gave us the most intense stare I have ever received from any living thing. Without thinking I pulled my small-caliber .22 pistol from its holster. Cocking the gun, I cautioned the others to stand very still.

Time seemed to stop as we waited for the bear to make his move.

Turning, with a quick swipe of a huge forepaw, he knocked over several aspen saplings standing in the way. Those saplings were three and four inches in diameter. Then he fled. Shaken, we moved to higher ground and sat down. Still holding the pistol, I realized how useless it would have been if brought against the strength of the animal we had just met.

An experience this dramatic needs expression. For a long time I told nearly everyone I met about the incident. To my delight, many of these people also

Meeting a huge brown bear, face to face, is always an exciting experience.

had their own bear stories to tell. Often they were hunting adventures or the details of some grisly bear attack they had recently heard about. But sometimes I heard stories about bears unaware of the person watching. These stories intrigued me, for they seemed to be glimpses into the mysterious, private world of bears.

As a boy I grew up steeped in the hunting traditions of the Old West. I was keen on bear stories and loved to hear tales about their behavior. By the time I graduated from high school and began to live on my own, I had gained a great deal of knowledge about bears. Unfortunately, as I learned while researching this book, most of it was wrong.

Anthropologist Margaret Mead used to say that misinformation is the world's most easily gotten commodity. This certainly seems to be the case when it comes to understanding bears. However, through stubborn persistence, aided by modern technology, wildlife biologists have learned more about bears during the last thirty years than in all of history. In part, this book is a compilation of what they have discovered.

But confusion and misconceptions die slowly. Even some of the words we use to discuss bears can be misleading. For example, male bears are often called "boars"; females, "sows"—terms used for pigs.

During the first quarter of this century, over 100 species of bears were thought to exist. Today, scientists recognize much less species diversification among bears. Only 8 species and perhaps 10 related subspecies are now "officially" acknowledged.

Common names like "grizzly" and "Alaskan brownie" cause further confusion. At least to me. It wasn't until I had worked nearly a year on this book that I began to sort them out. The term "grizzly" is a colloquialism for the inland race of the brown bear in North America *(Ursus arctos)*. The "Alaskan brownie" is a coastal variety of the same species. The differences between the two "races" are so vague that for management purposes the Alaska Fish and Game Department has arbitrarily drawn a line approximately 75 to 100 miles (120 to 160 km) inland from the coastline. Any *Ursus arctos* on the interior side of that line is referred to as a "grizzly." Any on the seaward side of that line is called an "Alaskan brown bear." To confound things further, some still believe the grizzly is a separate species or subspecies of brown bear. If so, then a "grizzly" bear wandering over a dividing mountain range in Alaska would change its species when it got to the other side.

In the beginning, as I researched this book, I thought I could be safe from confusion by using the bear's Latin "scientific" names. But because of periodic species renaming, those names proved to be just as bewildering as the common names. At one time, for example, polar bears carried the Latin name of *Thalassarctos maritimus*. Apparently this was during a period when biologists weren't really sure whether or not polar bears were really "bears." It was speculated that they might somehow be related to the weasel family. Polar bears officially reentered the bear family when they were given their new genus name, *Ursus maritimus*, the "sea bear." Also, until early in the 1960s, the American black bear carried the name *Euarctos americanus*. Today it is known as *Ursus americanus*.

Much of this standardization and streamlining of terms and information can be attributed to the formation of the International Bear Biology Association and the periodic conferences they hold. These bear conferences have enjoyed a brief but productive history. Beginning in 1968, a small group of biologists gathered for several days of informal talks in Whitehorse, Yukon Territory. Today, the conferences have expanded and are formally held every three years. Few wildlife species have received the magnitude of attention that has been directed toward bears in the last few decades.

All scientific names and terms included in this book are those currently in use. Although most of the information presented is generally accepted as fact, some biological concepts and behaviors are not well understood. In these cases, I will present one or two interpretations by other experts as well as my own. I hope that this book will act as a kind of catalyst for new thought as well as a good reference for what we already know.

To complete the three years of work that this book required, my cophotographer, Mark Newman, and I traveled over 120,000 miles, exposing some 800 rolls of film around the globe. I also tape-recorded and transcribed over 85 hours of interviews. Whenever I'm asked to comment on all the work involved in doing a book, my favorite reply is, "You don't just do a book . . . you live it." So it has been throughout this project.

Some of our methods of study were rather unorthodox for standard wildlife research. In Southeast Asia, for example, we carried out a campaign that became known as our "barroom research." For our study to succeed, we couldn't travel first class, and we couldn't stay in respectable hotels and eat at reputable restaurants. Instead, we constantly mixed with the locals, seeking out those who spoke even a tiny bit of English. Failing that, we brought out our little phrase books and pointed at sentences. And we bought people beer. Lots of beer. After we were feeling comfortable, we would pull out little pocket photos of the bears we were seeking information about.

At first, people were reluctant to tell us anything useful. But as the weeks passed, our reputation began to precede us and we started to be well received. For my report on the sun bear, this proved to be the crucial link. Almost nothing was known about their status or habits in the wild. Fortunately, our barroom research paid off, and we have a much better understanding of what the future may hold for these little bears of the jungle.

For additional data on the lesser-known "exotic" species of bears, I sent out dozens of research questionnaires to zoos around the world that keep bears. Since practically nothing has been written about these tropical animals, this was an attempt to learn something about their basic biology. The many replies that were returned to us have greatly aided our understanding of all bears.

Terry Domico
Bainbridge Island, Washington

ACKNOWLEDGMENTS

There were many, many people whose contributions directly or indirectly helped in the preparation of this book. I would like to give special tribute to a few without whose help this book may never have come into existence. Thanks to Dr. Charles Jonkel, for allowing our paths to cross so many times; to Ralph Flowers, for your attempts to make peace with the bears of Washington; to Lance Sundquist, conservation officer, British Columbia, for your campaign to keep the public informed about bears; to Larry Aumiller, for introducing me to the brown bears of McNeil River; to Polly Hessing, for sharing a rare sunny day at Mikfik Creek and for the neat bear skull that I received in the mail when I got home; to Bruce Kaye and the rest of the staff at Kenai Fjords National Park for helping Mark Newman survive the big storm; to Mark Rosenthal, Curator of Mammals at the Lincoln Park Zoo, for your help in photographing and understanding the spectacled bear; to Barrie Gilbert, for your continuing love of bears; to Kathleen Jope, for your help at Brooks Falls; to Bill Cook, for tolerating my persistent questions; to Bruce McLellan, for your memories of Blanche; to Pete Clarkson, for helping me survive the Tower; to Lance Olsen, for keeping me up on the *Bear News;* to Clifford Rice, for sharing your "proprietary" sloth bear info; to Wayne McCrory, for your diligence in Canadian conservation issues; to Cathy Peppers, for your translation of German publications into English; to Kenneth Elowe and Charles Willey, for your help in providing information and materials about the aging of bears; to the members of the International Bear Biology Association, for allowing me to wander freely through your meetings; to Lee Werle and David Towne of Seattle's Woodland Park Zoo, for helping Mark and me get into China; to Mike Craig, president of the Seattle-Chongqing Sister City Association, for helping us with Chinese contacts; to Tong Quixuo, panda keeper at the Chongqing Zoo, for being a patient photography assistant; to Toshihiro Hazumi, Tokyo Wildlife Management Office, for our talks about the art of life; to Naoko Maeda, Noboribetsu Bear Park, for your charming presence and dedication to your work; to Kazuhiko Maita, for my test of a lifetime; to Shin Yoshino, for your friendship and guidance in Tokyo; to Patrick Andau, game warden, Sabah, East Malaysia, for helping us work with sun bears; to Francis Liew and Diosdado Villanueva, Sabah Parks, as valued contacts; to Chin Kah Thing, who helped make all things in Borneo possible; to Ricky Lee, for sharing his pet sun bear with us; to Patrick Seah, Malaysian Airlines System employee, for helping us out of a taxi jam and for your continuing friendship; to Tiger Yang and Sun Shizheng, Chongqing Foreign Affairs Office, for your help in making our way through China; to Shi Ming Wen and Dr. Hu, of the Chongqing Zoo, for making your panda facilities available to us and for freely sharing your information; to Shi Liang, Chengdu Foreign Affairs Office, for a successful trip to Wolong; to William Thomas, Jr., U.S. consulate general, Chengdu, China, who "was a zoologist before he went wrong"; to Mark Newman, my cophotographer, for dedicating your time and talent to this project; to Ken Talley, for your valuable comments about the text; to my agent, Ivy Stone, from whose idea this project evolved; and to my editor, Gerry Helferich, for your helpful guidance. Because of all these people, I have grown.

Note by Mark Newman

In 1981, I moved my family from Wyoming to Alaska in order to be closer to what was truly wild in North America. As a wildlife photographer in this great northland, it took me very little time to realize that it was the grizzly bear, more than any other species, that embodied the very essence of the wilderness feeling that I hungered for. Thus when Terry Domico called me in the winter of 1985 to ask if I wanted to collaborate with him on a book about bears, his question was hardly necessary.

Little did I know that within two years of that phone call, I would be on my hands and knees in the jungles of Borneo, pulling leeches off my body while at the same time trying to snap pictures of the Malaysian sun bear; or having an orangutan grab me in the equatorial rain forest and walk me down the trail for two hundred yards before letting go; or drinking murky water mixed with elephant urine from jungle mudholes to quench my thirst and prevent dehydration; or engaging in survival bicycling among a million people in downtown Chengdu, China, while awaiting permit clearance to the Wolong Panda Preserve; or risking "survival" dining, a sport in its own right, when the menu says snakes or eels, and says it in a foreign language; or freezing to near-death at −100°F in gale-force winds in Manitoba while attempting to capture images of cold-oblivious polar bears; or getting stranded, alone, on an Alaskan beach during a two-week marathon rainstorm, trying to photograph coastal black bears while the raging surf crashed nonstop, washing up dead seals and porpoises right behind my tent.

Thanks for everything, Terry.

Mark Newman
Anchorage, Alaska

BEARS
of the
WORLD

BEING A BEAR:

The Secret Life of Bruin

Like nearly everyone who goes into the forest alone, I'm afraid of bears . . . or, rather, I was until one special evening about midnight in southwest Alaska's Katmai National Park. I had come there to photograph brown bears as they fished for migrating salmon at Brooks Falls. The photo I wanted was from an underwater point of view, so I had previously designed and constructed a submersible "robot" camera that could be remotely controlled.

Every day I would place the camera in the plunge pool at the base of the falls where salmon were concentrated and hope a bear would perform within camera range. Since it was summer in Alaska, the sun stayed up almost until midnight. After sunset I would pull the camera out of the river, stow it in a duffel bag, throw the bag over my shoulder, and hike the two-mile-long trail back to camp.

On this particular evening, an off-duty park ranger was assisting me. We had finished the day's attempt for an underwater photo and were walking along the trail, chatting. Every now and then we would call out to the forest, "Hey bear!" to warn any bears of our approach.

As we rounded a bend, we suddenly encountered a large mother brown bear lying with two cubs in the middle of the trail. For some reason the bear hadn't heard us; perhaps she had been asleep. Park rangers had warned me earlier that to approach closer than 50 or 60 yards (46 or 55 m) to one of these big bears is really pushing your safety limits, especially if the bear has cubs. Often that "bubble" of intruder sensitivity that surrounds a bear extends over 100 yards (92 m) out from the animal. This bear was hardly 40 feet (12 m) away from us.

We both stopped in our tracks and assessed the situation. The trail split into two directions a few feet in front of the bears. They were blocking the left fork

Bear prints in soft mud clearly show five toes on each foot. The uppermost print, with the elongated heel, was made by the bear's hind foot.

Although this mother brown bear is displaying ignoring behavior, her two half-grown cubs keep a wary eye on the photographer.

that went to the bridge. The right fork, which led to a small boat used to cross the nearby river, was much too close to the bears to be attempted. So, as we discussed our predicament, we began softly walking backward. It was then the mother bear rose to her feet, facing us. We stopped moving and talked softly to her. She looked from one to the other of us and then turned and walked over to the river. Casting an over-the-shoulder glance at us, she called her cubs, then put her head down below the bank and began splashing the water with her paw. All we could see was her great, shaggy rear end.

Now, it seems to me that a bear who is agitated by our presence isn't going to present her rear end to us. This bear was letting us pass. As we turned that right-hand corner on the trail to the boat I twisted my neck, trying to keep an eye on the bear. A bit further up the trail I glanced back again; the bear was watching us. A moment later she lumbered back to her spot in the middle of the trail and lay down, cubs clamoring around her. I had a strong feeling that we had just met an intelligent wild being.

Later, I mentioned this incident to Barrie Gilbert, an authority on bear behavior at Utah State University, who was studying bear/people interactions at Katmai National Park in Alaska. I asked him whether he believed that the bear had sized up the situation and then let us go by. Barrie responded that this behavior is common enough to even have a name—''ignoring behavior.'' Apparently the bear had determined that we weren't threatening her or her cubs. The best way she could disarm the situation was to put her head down, out of sight.

The stuff of nightmares, a curious bear's eyes glow in the light of a campfire.

''She was essentially saying to you, 'I'm not looking, so get going,' '' Barrie explained.

This was the first time I had ever encountered a wild animal that displayed a sense of discretion. Most of my fear of bears had suddenly been replaced by a great deal of respect.

That newfound respect made me want to know about bears and their evolutionary history. Just what are the qualities that make a bear?

BEAR BEGINNINGS

Facts about the beginnings of the bear tribe are sketchy. Apparently, about 30 to 40 million years ago, during the early portion of the Oligocene epoch, bears began to evolve from a family of small, carnivorous, tree-climbing mammals called miacids. Coyotes, wolves, foxes, raccoons, and dogs are also thought to have evolved from this ancestral stock. Very early in their history the miacids developed special teeth for piercing and tearing flesh—the canine teeth. The early carnivores developed other special teeth called carnassials. The last premolar in the upper jaw and the first molar in the lower jaw were modified to act like scissors, shearing meat into easily swallowed chunks.

At first, the brains of these carnivores were small, perhaps because those early herbivores on which they fed could be caught without much trouble. (Through time, in an evolutionary "arms race," both predator and prey developed bigger brains and more complex behavior patterns in order to outwit each other often enough for continued survival of their species.)

Meat eating became a highly successful occupation for carnivores, and they quickly radiated into three main branches: the dog, the cat, and seal families. The first true bears evolved from the tribe of heavy bearlike dogs that existed in North America during the late Oligocene epoch, some 27 million years ago.

According to some researchers, the oldest known bear, *Ursavus elemensis*, was about the size of a fox terrier. It lived about 20 million years ago in a subtropical Europe. Bears came into their own about 6 million years ago and quickly evolved into numerous forms. Some grew to enormous size. Then, because of widespread changes, probably climatic, nine genera and numerous bear species became extinct. Somewhere during this time our modern line of bears developed from a little bear known as Protursus, which also died out in time.

The structure of this massive brown-bear skull clearly illustrates its carnivorous nature and its kinship with dogs.

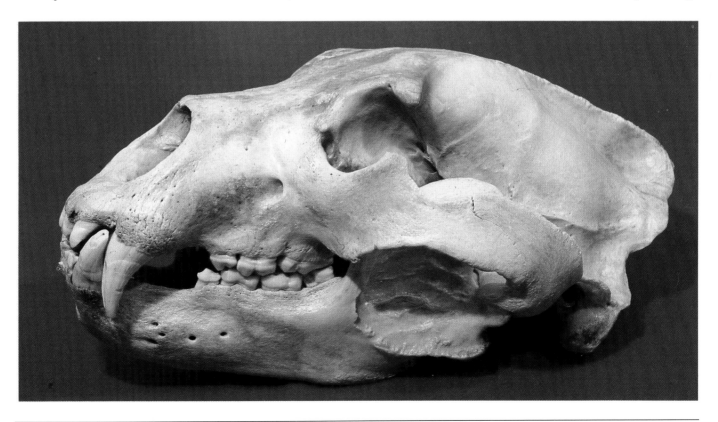

The Rise and Fall of the Third Bear

About 2.5 million years ago the first of the genus *Ursus* (Latin for bear) appeared. From its European descendants came the Etruscan bear, *Ursus etruscus*, which later separated into three distinct lines. Two of these lines were found in Asia, and it is thought that they lead to today's brown bears and black bears. The third line, now extinct, lived in Europe, and is known as the cave bear, *Ursus spelaus*. Cave bears were contemporaries of early humans, who probably hunted them for food. Fossil remains of cave bears span the period from 30,000 or 40,000 (maybe even 50,000) years to about 10,000 years ago.

Just why the cave bear died out is a subject of great speculation among paleontologists. Some assert that the bear perished of its own "self-domestication" from prolonged internment during the long Ice Age winters. When large predators are kept for many years in the confinement of cages, peculiar diseases of the spinal column develop. These include inflammations, fusing, and atrophy. An extraordinarily large number of cave bear remains are from diseased or physically degenerate bears.

Also extraordinary are the numbers of cave bear skeletons that have been discovered. The most impressive find was in Dragon's Cave at Mixnitz in Aus-

Adapted to a hostile world of ice, the polar bear is considered the world's most recently evolved ursine species.

Bears also have color vision of some kind. Dr. Jonkel has found that bears are attracted to colors, but it's not clear to him whether or not it was the actual color or its shading that the bears were responding to. "Not much investigation has been done on this subject, but color perception is usually an indicator of a visually keen animal," he says. Bears are active both in daylight and at night. This is another indication of good eyesight.

The very arrangement of the eyes in the face tells us something about a bear's vision. Carnivores have their eyes set relatively close together and facing forward, for more effective depth perception and prey location. A good predator obviously needs good eyes to track moving prey.

Evidence of Excellent Eyesight

Experiments in 1937 showed that brown bears in a European zoo could recognize their keeper at 100 yards (91 m). Recently, in the Chengdu Zoo in China, I watched as hundreds of visitors tossed pieces of food to several bears who were making begging postures. Peanuts, crackers, bits of bread, chunks of candy, all were tossed some 20 to 30 feet (6 to 9 m) to the bears waiting in the pit below. As each missile arched into the compound, a nearby bear would casually lean out and deftly snap it from the air. Sometimes nonfood items were also tossed—coins, pebbles, sticks. What surprised me was that the bears apparently could determine the edibility of an object flying toward them—few of the bears would snap at those inedible "ringers."

Bears are very good at detecting movement, even at long distances, as I accidentally learned one morning. For ten days and nights I had been sitting in a rented car watching bear traffic come and go at a municipal dump in northern Canada. My morning watch normally began at 3:30 A.M. and would continue until about 10:30 A.M., when bear activity would practically cease.

One morning I sat there among the buzzing flies, with the window open, my elbow on the sill, my hand gripping the edge of the car's roof where it meets the upper door. Approximately 200 to 300 feet (60 to 90 m) away were eight adult black bears scrounging through the garbage. As I watched, remaining very still, a fly lit on the finger of my hand that was holding onto the roof. I moved the finger to chase it away. Immediately, nearly every bear on the dump lifted its head to look at me. They must have caught the movement in their peripheral vision.

How the Bad-Vision Myth Came to Be (Maybe)

As I watched those bears at the dump, I came to realize that peripheral vision may play a large part in a bear's relationship with other bears and in encounters with people. Often when two bears approached on the dump, they would try not to look directly at each other. Instead they would avert their gazes off to the side, sometimes even turning their heads slightly. Perhaps a direct stare amounts to a direct threat in bear society. In order to defuse the situation and let other bears pass close by, a kind of "ignoring behavior" was in play. Only when an offending bear had approached too closely did the two bears look directly at each other. Often this preceded one, usually the larger bear, chasing the other away from the dump.

During encounters with people, nonaggressive bears often seem to use this averted gaze in the hopes of avoiding trouble. This may lead to a mistaken impression that the bear doesn't see the person. When the bear does finally turn and look at someone directly, it's because they are too close for comfort, especially if that person is also staring back. Usually the bear makes the intelligent move and withdraws.

BEAR INTELLIGENCE

Just how intelligent are these animals? Bear intelligence cannot be measured in human terms, but they do exhibit a great deal of curiosity. Biologists believe curiosity is an evolved characteristic that helps bears discover the most productive and nutritious foods. But bears' curiosity is not limited to food. Often they will approach and investigate any new object they find in their environment. Like humans, bears have a wide range of behavior to choose from when faced with different situations. In this way they can be quite unpredictable.

Animal trainer Doug Seus, of Heber City, Utah, trains bears, wolves, and cougars for the motion picture industry. He reports that brown bears, especially grizzlies and Kodiaks, are the hardest to tame but the easiest to train. Generally, he has to teach them something only once.

This single-trial learning is another indicator of bear intelligence. If a bear wandering along a trail finds a bit of chocolate in a discarded candy bar wrapper, he will remember that incident for months. He may make several visits back to that spot, just in case another candy bar turns up.

Bears will also seek out resting positions where they can watch hunters or human intruders without being seen. Lance Olsen, director of Montana's Great Bear Foundation, points out that an animal's self-concealment may imply conscious thinking and self-awareness. Many bear hunters know that a pursued bear will often make an effort to avoid leaving tracks.

Wildlife biologist Bruce McLellan once encountered a female black bear that repeatedly avoided being caught in his live traps. Each time a trap was set, the bear would roll a large rock into it, setting off the trigger mechanism. Then she would eat the meat used as bait. After several days of this, the bear began hanging around in nearby trees, waiting for McLellan and his assistant to bait the trap and leave. Only by setting up a dummy trap ringed with hidden snares were they finally able to catch her.

FOOD STRATEGIES

Northern bears have a terrific motivation to gain weight. Since much of their year is spent asleep in hibernation, they have only a short active period in which to find enough food to survive the winter. Much of a bear's waking time is spent solving the problem of getting food, the more nutritious the better. For example, bears prefer to eat plants when they are at the peak of protein content—usually during preflowering or early flowering stages.

If food becomes extremely abundant, such as during a salmon run in Alaska, bears may become selective about what portions of the fish they eat. Hungry bears will eat the entire salmon. They prefer, however, to eat the eggs of female salmon, which are extremely rich in nutrition. When a bear catches a salmon it determines at once whether it is a male or female. If salmon are plentiful, the bear will often abandon the males and resume fishing in hope of catching a female salmon.

A bear normally spends its time in a series of small areas where it can find food. Collectively, these areas make up its home range. It moves around within this range in order to take advantage of seasonal food sources. The routes to and from these areas of use are often called travel lanes. Although bears will use human roads, 95 percent of their travel is off-road, particularly in swamps and forests.

Homing Instinct

If a bear is removed from its home range it will display an extraordinary homing instinct. In Michigan, an adult male black bear homed after being transplanted by air for a distance of 156 miles (251 km). Twelve adult Alaskan brown bears returned to their capture sites in an average of fifty-eight days. They all had been transplanted over 125 miles (201 km) away.

One of the most remarkable examples of homing was that of a young brown bear captured near Cordova, Alaska, in September 1973. This bear was transplanted by boat to Montague Island in Prince William Sound, a direct distance of nearly 58 miles (93 km). Twenty-eight days later the same bear was killed within 109 yards (100 m) of its capture site. The return route must have required swimming some 7 miles (11.3 km) to Hinchinbrook Island, then a .5-mile (1-km) swim to Hawkins Island, and a 1.75-mile (2.8-km) swim to the mainland. All this was accomplished at right angles to strong tides and in the frigid waters of Prince William Sound. Incidents like this drove scientists to conclude that transplanting nuisance brown bears was an unreliable management procedure.

Hibernation

A bear's instinct to den is an adaptation to life in places where winter conditions might otherwise threaten survival. For some unknown reason, a few individuals of a hibernating species may remain active all winter even though no food may be available. Normally, the problems of reduced food supply, decreased mobility because of deep snow, and the increased energy costs of keeping warm are solved by denning and hibernation.

Northern bears usually choose a low cave, a hollow tree, or the shelter of a brush pile as a den site in which to hibernate. Sometimes an earthen den is dug directly into the ground. Often the den chamber is lined with dried grasses and leaves to make an insulated bed.

Denning time generally coincides with the first inclement winter weather, although the disappearance of high-quality food determines the actual time of denning. During late summer, bears have been known to eat as much as 20,000 calories a day in a final effort to accumulate enough fat reserves for hibernation. This is equivalent to a human eating thirty-eight banana splits or forty-two hamburgers each day. Most zoo bears, when regularly fed throughout the winter, do not den.

During the last days before hibernation, some kinds of bears will eat certain indigestible materials—resinous plants and fibers—which form a mass in the rectum and plug the anus. The function of the anal plug is not well understood.

Biologists differ as to whether or not bears enter a state of true hibernation, but the controversy may be largely a matter of terminology. Many smaller mammals, such as chipmunks and marmots, enter a deep sleep from which they cannot be easily aroused. While they are dormant, their body temperatures are considerably lower than normal. A hibernating bear's temperature, in contrast, does not drop more than about 9° F (5° C) from its normal 87.8° to 99° F (31° to 37.4° C). Bears can be easily awakened, but if undisturbed, they may sleep for as long as a month without changing position.

Hibernating bears can remain in their dens from two and a half to seven months, depending on climate, without eating food, drinking water, urinating,

Seen at the entrance of its den, a brown bear, like many northern bears, prepares to spend the winter in hibernation. The strategy is an excellent way to avoid long, dangerous foraging periods when little food is available.

or defecating. Smaller mammals, however, must wake up periodically to eat and expel body wastes.

Bears accomplish this amazing fast through their unique metabolic system. During hibernation the water content of their blood remains at a constant level. Minor losses of water are balanced by the breakdown of fat reserves. Although a small amount of urea is continually formed, it is quickly degraded by a refined system that recycles nitrogen and prevents toxic uremia. Knowledge about these metabolic systems is helping researchers to develop special diets for humans with kidney problems and diabetes.

During winter hibernation a bear burns about 4,000 calories a day. Although its heart rate drops to about eight beats per minute, compared to from forty to fifty beats per minute during summer sleep, its oxygen consumption rate may drop only to about 50 percent of that of an active bear. Bears also have been known to shiver in order to generate enough heat to keep warm during hibernation.

When bears leave their dens in the springtime, it may take weeks before they resume their normal intake of food. Apparently, these metabolic adjustments of hibernation persist for some time after they have become active again.

Daybeds

Bears sometimes construct daybeds during spring and summer. They usually are simply trampled spots in bushes or shallow pits dug into the ground. These beds are often located near food sources and are probably used for resting after a heavy meal. Sometimes they are located high on a hill or bluff, hidden, but with a commanding view for keeping watch over the area.

REPRODUCTION

Bears mate like dogs. Mounting the female from the rear, the male often holds her by clasping his forelimbs around her waist. Copulation may last from one to twenty minutes, depending on species and individuals.

Mating dog-fashion, these brown bears may copulate several times a day during the short breeding season.

Among northern bears, birth of young takes place during the winter sleep. (Southern species, which do not hibernate, can give birth at any time of the year.) Although mating may have occurred in late spring or early summer, a survival mechanism, known as delayed implantation, ensures that the fertilized egg does not implant in the wall of the uterus until October or November. The blastocyst, that little, hollow ball of cells resulting from the growth of a fertilized ovum, "free floats" in the female reproductive tract for as long as five months. During this time the embryo's development is halted.

Because of the bear's denning habit, all the nutritional demands of pregnancy and early lactation occur when the female is not taking in any food. If the bear is in poor physical condition, or does not find sufficient food, the fertilized egg will not implant. This mechanism saves the bear from additional stress that might threaten its survival. Some other animals, such as mink, bats, armadillos, kangaroos, and red deer, have developed similar delayed implantation strategies.

Assuming a pregnant bear is healthy, with plenty of fat reserves, then the little blastocyst will implant for a short gestation period ranging from six to eight weeks. This brief development time means that the cubs are surprisingly small at birth.

A newborn brown bear weighs about 1/720th as much as its mother—10 ounces (283 g) compared to 450 pounds (204 kg). (A newborn human child's weight is about 1/20th that of the mother.)

The tiny cubs are blind when born. Covered with very fine hair, they look almost naked. As they nurse, they are kept warm by their mother's body. When

Delayed embryo implantation ensures that these American black bear cubs will be able to spend their first weeks secure in their mother's hibernation den. (Dennis McAllister)

the little bears are old enough to accompany her into the outside world, their eyes will be open and their fur thick and warm.

Usually the females have the sole responsibility for raising the young. They are devoted mothers, too, always ready to fight if they think the cubs are in danger. Often the greatest danger to young bears are adult male bears, who sometimes try to eat them. In some localities nearly 40 percent of the cubs are killed by other bears. Over the long run this harassing and occasional killing of young bears is believed to be beneficial to the entire bear population by naturally regulating overcrowding.

Forever at risk from large aggressive male bears, this little brown bear cub must stay extremely close to its mother for the first few months of its life.

Behavior of the Social Bear

Bears have long been described as solitary animals, living their lives in isolation except during a brief mating season. But this picture is slowly changing. The family is the bear's basic social unit. Young bears usually spend the first two or three years of life accompanied by their mothers and one or more siblings. Because female bears normally reproduce every two or three years, most of their lives are spent in the company of other bears. Even after separation from their mother, siblings may feed and travel together for a few more years.

Adult bears get together, most often as mating pairs, for two or three weeks during the annual breeding season. They also gather within growling distance of each other around rich food sources such as large carcasses, fish-spawning streams, or garbage dumps. Every autumn, polar bears concentrate along the northern coast of Hudson Bay while waiting for the ice to form.

Almost too large to nurse, this half-grown brown bear will probably be weaned and on its own before long.

The Dominance Hierarchy

In general, bears are shy animals that usually try to avoid trouble. When two bears meet, a hierarchy usually prevents the really fierce encounter that could result in serious injury or death. In a series of short fights or by ritualized threat displays, the largest bears test each other's strength and determine which ones are dominant. (Scars found on older bears reveal that a fair amount of real fighting does occur.)

Dominance is usually a matter of size and sex; males are dominant over females, except those with cubs. Male bears will often defer to a female with cubs because they know that she will defend them to the death.

When several bears are feeding together, say, at a salmon stream, their mutual tolerance is maintained by the dominance hierarchy. The order is usually maintained by posturing and head movements. An aggressive signal might include staring, loud roaring, or "mouthing"—the waving of an open mouth near the head of a bear that approached too closely. Sitting or running are submissive gestures. Generally speaking, the larger the bear, the wider the berth its fellows give it.

I mentioned earlier that I once camped in a rented car for ten days in order

Arguing in midwater, possibly over fishing rights, one of these bears will eventually establish dominance through ritualized combat.

to study black bears visiting a municipal dump. The bears' pecking order became evident after only a few days. Unknowingly, the people who used the dump became part of the dominance hierarchy equation. The biggest bears fed in the dump at the most desirable hours of late evening and early morning, when human traffic had stopped. Subadults and females with cubs scrounged food at the dump in late morning and early evening, when the dump was used only lightly by people. Two half-grown, apparently orphaned, cubs would use the dump during midday, when the bulldozer was at work pushing in landfill. This was the only time of the day when no other bears were present, and the cubs found refuge by feeding near the human activity, which was keeping the bigger, potentially dangerous bears away. Apparently, those subadults and females with cubs considered people less of a threat than the dominant males. Conversely, the presence of a person seemed to make those big bears extremely nervous.

Recent evidence suggests that bears react to people just as if they were encountering another, slightly superior, bear. Juvenile bears, when around people, usually get involved in more dominance confrontations than older bears do. This may be because these younger bears are still trying to establish their place in the dominance hierarchy. Older bears who "realize" that people and their weapons are the ultimate dominant "bears" may be the bears who live longest.

AMERICAN BLACK BEARS:

America's Most Familiar Bears

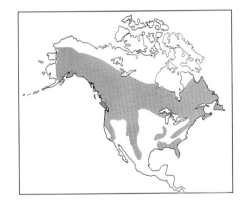

American black bears are the most widespread and numerous bears in North America. They inhabit most of the continent's forested areas, beginning at the northern tree limit of the Arctic, south throughout much of the United States, and down the wooded Sierra Madre Mountains into northern Mexico. East and west, they range from Newfoundland to British Columbia's Queen Charlotte Islands.

HABITAT PREFERENCES AND RELATIVE ABUNDANCE

In all parts of their range, black bears prefer forests with intermittent open areas (meadows) that provide them with numerous berries and other desirable foods. They are most abundant in the mixed hardwood forests of the East and in the vast coniferous forests rimming the Pacific Northwest. They are least common on the Great Plains. It is difficult to accurately determine the number of black bears alive today. Some of our best estimates place the total population for all of North America somewhere between 400,000 and 750,000. (Because these estimates come from scientists, the numbers are probably rather conservative.)

CONFUSING COLORS, CONFUSING NAMES

To the early settlers who pioneered the eastern part of North America, the name "black bear" was an obvious choice. Nearly all the bears in this region have

Highly adaptable, black bears are the most widespread and successful bears in North America.

Previous page: Mixed hardwood and coniferous forests having intermittent open areas are prime black bear habitat. (Mel Douglas)

Often called "cinnamon bears", black bears west of the Mississippi River commonly have a brown color phase.

black coats with brown eyes and brown muzzles. But as the white man pushed west, people began to encounter bears that resembled black bears in nearly every way except they had rusty brown fur. These bears became known as "cinnamon bears" and for a long time were thought to be a separate species. Eventually, these brown bears were discovered to be only a color variation of the more common black bear. Cinnamon-colored cubs are frequently born into litters containing black ones.

Black bears can be a variety of colors ranging from black (of course) to cinnamon, beige, white, and even blue. Around the turn of the century, each time a new color phase was discovered it was thought a new species had been found. The case of the "glacier" bear is typical. The glacier bear is a bluish bear found only in a limited area within the glaciated mountains of the Saint Elias Range in southeastern Alaska. These bears have a remarkable color similarity to the icy world they inhabit, making them very difficult to see. A few skins, brought out from that region by hunters, convinced naturalists that this was a new species. Years later, after careful examination of live specimens, the blue bear is considered to be just another guise of the ubiquitous "black bear."

According to Gary Vequist, resource manager for Glacier Bay National Park, the blue "glacier bear" color phase is very rare today. Apparently these bears have bred with other color phase bears, resulting in offspring without the bluish tint.

The Case of the White Black Bears

Probably the most dramatic color variation of the "black bear" is the Kermode bear. Found only in three small, isolated areas of coastal British Columbia, these bears have beautiful cream-colored fur. To some, they resemble polar bears who have been airlifted out of their arctic habitat and simply dropped off in the dense forests that cover the region. In addition to white, Kermodes can also be chestnut red, bright yellow, blue-gray, or even orange. Their eyes are brown, confirming that this is definitely not a race of albino bears.

Almost mystical in appearance, a rare Kermode bear surveys its domain from a large tree on Canada's west coast.

Kermode bears were first described to science in 1905 by Dr. William Hornaday of the New York Zoo. Hornaday considered them a distinct species and named them *Ursus kermodei* after his Canadian colleague, Francis Kermode, in recognition of his efforts to secure specimens and information. Later, in 1928, it was determined that the Kermode bear was only a geographic race of the ''black bear.''

Today, strict Canadian laws have outlawed any hunting of these beautiful bears. Although they are rarely seen, Kermode bears are revered by nearly all the local people living within their range. During a photographic expedition to this region, I watched a Native couple become highly excited when they saw their first Kermode bear. They explained to me that they had lived in the area all their lives and had never before seen the so-called ghost bear.

Should We Rename the ''Black Bear''?

With all these color phases of American ''black bears'' running around, perhaps it would be wise for us to rename the species. *Ursus americanus*, its Latin name, means ''American bear.'' What other name could be simpler or more obvious? This species is found only in North America, so ''American bear'' would be accurate. Maybe the idea, given enough time, will finally catch on.

Color Phases May Help Bears Live a Little Better

Very little research has been aimed at understanding the color phases of American ''black bears.'' The few studies on ''cinnamon'' bears have revealed some surprising facts, however.

''Brown phase black bears seem to occur mostly in a large arc of territory extending roughly from northern California to central Manitoba,'' explains Dr. Charles Jonkel, a bear specialist with the University of Montana. ''Within that band some 40 percent to 60 percent (depending on where you are) of the black bears will be brown.''

Dr. Jonkel studied the bear's use of south-facing slopes in a portion of Montana's Rocky Mountains. In many areas, south-facing slopes have exposed areas called ''balds,'' which, in the spring, can be important food sources to bears that have recently emerged from hibernation. The snow cover usually melts first on these slopes, allowing the earliest food plants to sprout and green up from the warmth of the soil and spring sun. Bears know this and come here to forage.

''By midday, even in May, these south-facing slopes can get as hot as hell,'' Dr. Jonkel continues. ''I found that the brown and lighter-colored bears could stay out on the hillside to feed much longer than the black ones could.''

Dr. Jonkel thinks that the ability to feed longer on these south-facing balds favors the brown color phase in this area.

In the cool, moist forests of Washington State's Olympic Peninsula, spring overheating is not a problem. There, the bear population is 100 percent black colored. But only 100 miles (160 km) away, in the nearby Cascade Mountains, which are drier, nearly 60 percent of the bears have brown fur.

Dr. Jonkel comments on this:

> Some kind of very strong selection process for brown color must be in operation here. If you look around Minnesota, you will find very few brown ''black'' bears; get to Michigan and you will find none. All through the eastern states of New York, Pennsylvania, etc., you won't see any brown ones . . . for some reason they're just not favored there.

FOOD HABITS

Whatever its color, the American black bear is a four-legged garbage grinder when it comes to eating. Everything in the forest is fair game. In the course of a day they may feed on berries, animal carcasses, dead fish washed up on the shore of a lake, ants and other insects, acorns and beechnuts, wild cherries, honey (which they are extremely fond of), grass and herbs—practically anything edible. Research has shown, however, that these bears subsist mainly as vegetarians. Less than 25 percent of their diet is composed of animal matter.

Their food habits vary greatly with seasonal availability and location. Black bears on the West Coast live primarily on berries, fish, and marine invertebrates found along beaches and in tidal pools. In Alaska, black bears kill moose calves and fish for salmon. In northern Canada they eat lemmings when they can catch them.

Food is a frequent cause of contention between black bears and people. These extremely intelligent and rather shy bears are the only bear species in North America that has adapted to civilization. To these bears, people and their belongings often mean just one thing—food. Cabins, camps, food caches, garbage cans, and town dumps are often raided by bears looking for an easy meal. It's amazing the amount of damage a hungry bear can do to a house or truck camper when it is trying to get in. I have seen entire walls ripped to splinters by bears who smelled food on the other side.

Panhandling and Muggings in the National Parks

Many of the black bears in America's national parks panhandle food from well-intentioned but misinformed visitors. Park officials wage a continuous campaign to discourage bear feeding. In the Great Smokies National Park, dangerous traffic jams caused by begging bears are a daily occurrence. Some park bears go a step

Human garbage provides a nutritious food source for a large bear. All too often, bears that become accustomed to eating human food get into trouble when they expand their foraging activities to include cabins, food caches, camps, and picnics.

An Alaskan black bear splashes through a stream in an effort to catch a fleeing salmon.

A bear visiting an evening campsite in the Great Smokies National Park is not just looking for a handout—it will take the whole meal if it can reach it.

further and become aggressive about getting food from tourists. Picnic tables and ice chests are the usual targets, but some bears have resorted to "mugging" parked cars to get at food left inside. It's a nasty surprise when the owner of a vehicle returns from a hike and finds the windows broken out or the car door peeled from its hinges by brute strength.

A ranger from Yosemite National Park in California told me about one particularly smart bear that specialized in mugging Volkswagens. Apparently, the bear discovered that Volkswagens are air tight when their doors are locked and the windows rolled up. The bear would climb onto the roof of the car and jump up and down a few times, caving in the roof. As the roof collapsed, the resulting air pressure inside would make the doors pop open. Dinner is served! This technique became so successful that the bear began mugging nearly every unattended Volkswagen it found.

Most black bears are well behaved, however, preferring to avoid people and their property. But once they develop a taste for human food or garbage, they can seldom be persuaded to forgo it. All too often this results in a conflict wherein the bear is shot to protect property and ensure human safety. Park rangers quickly disposed of the Volkswagen-mugging bear mentioned above.

VITAL STATISTICS

Black bears are the smallest of the North American bears. On the average, adults stand from 35 to 40 inches (89 to 102 cm) high when on all fours and from 4.5 to 6 feet (1.37 to 1.82 m) in length, including a short tail some 5 inches (13 cm) long. Weights are highly variable, ranging from 125 to over 600 pounds (57 to 272 kg). Size and weight vary considerably and depend on food availability in the area where the bear lives. Males are usually about a third larger than females.

Incidentally, most people who encounter bears infrequently will grossly overestimate a bear's weight, usually by a factor of two. Black bears have a lot of long fur and "emotionally" look larger-than-life.

The only other bear that might be confused with the black bear is the inland variety of brown bear called the "grizzly." One feature that distinguishes the black bear from its rather aggressive cousin is its more horizontal shoulder-to-rump line. Grizzlies usually have a distinct shoulder hump. Also, grizzlies often

In Wyoming, a brown-phase black bear feeds on the carcass of a deer. (Larry Thorngren)

Although smaller than its cousin the brown bear, a black bear standing in a certain position will appear to have a shoulder hump much like a grizzly's. The shorter claws of the black bear are rarely visible, however, even at close range.

show a whitish, "grizzled" coloration over the shoulders. This is rarely seen in black bears, although a patch of white is often seen on the chest. In bright sunlight a black bear's coat may appear glossy; that of a grizzly never does. Sometimes the claws can be another good field mark. Black bears have relatively short claws. If its claws can be seen while the animal is walking, then be especially careful; most likely you are looking at a grizzly bear.

HOME ON THE BLACK BEAR RANGE

Every adult black bear has an individual territory. Home ranges may overlap, but a small core area is usually maintained by each bear as its exclusive domain. Mature males establish a perennial "mating range," which includes the home ranges of several females. In general, males maintain home ranges about four times larger than those of females. Bear home ranges generally vary in size from 2.5 to 10 square miles (6.4 to 25.9 sq km) for females and from 10 to over 52 square miles (26 to 132 sq km) for miles. Available food and population density seem to be major factors in determining the size of an individual bear's range.

The family unit of a mother with cubs begins to break up when the cubs are about a year and a half old. Usually these subadult bears leave the area to wander around, eventually establishing their own territories in vacant areas. But occasionally a mother will share her own range with a female offspring, who will take over the area should the mother die.

Black bears choose their travel lanes rather carefully. Usually they will avoid open areas, remaining near the edge of the woods' cover. In populated areas they will use stream beds as travel lanes because the creeks provide dense cover and a handy escape route. Black bears are capable of speeds of up to 30 miles per hour (50 kph) but seldom run unless they have to. When alarmed, black bears will often climb a tree for safety. Black bears may have developed this tree-climbing ability to escape predation from brown bears, which are not as arboreal.

BEAR TREES

Visual signs other than tracks are left by black bears. One of the most intriguing is scratch marks left on certain trees. The bears are said to also rub themselves on these trees. One set of claw marks I examined in the eastern Cascades Mountains of Washington State extended from 9 feet (2.74 m) up a poplar tree, nearly to the ground.

Black-bear biologist Lynn Rogers may have uncovered the reason for this behavior. He feels that dominant male bears in aggressive moods mark trees so that other males will be alerted and avoid mutually damaging conflicts. Studies have shown that the marking frequency is greatest just prior and during the breeding season. Tree marking might also promote estrus (the time when a female is ready to conceive) in adult females living in the area. This would also explain the high frequency of marking several weeks prior to the breeding season.

BLACK BEAR REPRODUCTION

Mating usually takes place in May and June, but in northern climates it can be as late as July or August. Females are sexually mature from three to five years of age, but some do not mate until age seven. In areas where bears are heavily hunted, females may begin reproducing in their third year. Copulation is dog-fashion, lasting from fifteen to thirty minutes. Individual females are visited regularly by males for two- or three-week periods during the breeding season. Most meetings are brief, lasting only a few hours, as the males assess the females' readiness. Black bear females normally breed every other year.

In the uterus, the fertilized ovum divides a few times and then floats free for about six months, its development arrested. Delayed implantation occurs around October, and after about an eight-week gestation period the cubs are born in January or February while the mother is still in the den. If the mother does not have enough fat reserves, she won't implant, and the embryos get ''scrubbed'' and reabsorbed by the body.

Usually two cubs are born, but some litters may only contain one or as many as four. The cubs, which weigh somewhere between 8.5 and 11.5 ounces (240 to 330 g) are blind, nearly hairless, and totally helpless at birth. A human baby having the same relation to its mother's weight would weigh only about 5 ounces (142 g).

At first, black bear cubs' hindquarters are so underdeveloped that they have to move around the den by pulling themselves along with their front legs. By the time the cubs are five weeks old they are strong enough to walk. When they are ready to leave the den in the spring, they can easily follow their mother about.

TOUGH TIMES FOR BABY BLACK BEARS

The first few months of life outside the den are perilous for the young cubs. One study showed that the majority of cub mortality occurs within sixty days after den emergence. Large male bears are the greatest danger, but little cubs are also occasionally eaten by eagles, bobcats, and mountain lions. Mother bears will often move out of the area after they have lost their cubs.

In recent years, researchers have successfully introduced a series of orphaned black bear cubs to foster mothers still in hibernation. The natural mothers of the unfortunate cubs had either been killed or driven away from their dens while the cubs were still only a few weeks old. During one experiment, five out of seven cubs were confirmed as accepted after den emergence.

After emergence, a mother must be especially careful to protect her cubs from possible harm. When she has to leave them so she can feed, she will sometimes make a nest under a large tree to serve as shelter for the cubs. If threatened while out in the woods, the cubs will quickly climb the nearest tree while the mother stands guard nearby. They also spend a good deal of time in trees playing or just resting and sunbathing.

By the time they are six months old, the cubs may weigh 55 to 65 pounds (25 to 30 kg). Although they are capable of fending for themselves, they usually den with their mother during the next winter. The following spring she often forces them to shift for themselves.

Young bears are extremely vulnerable during their first year alone, and mortality then is high. Large male bears often harass them, and with their lack of foraging experience they are easily attracted to dumps and garbage cans for food scraps. Many end up being shot as nuisances.

Alaskan wildlife researcher Dennis McAllister holds four squirming month-old black bear cubs. This unusually large litter indicates that the mother, which has been tranquilized, is in excellent health and has been finding more than adequate nutrition during the active season. (Jack Whitman)

THE HIBERNATING BLACK BEAR

As fall approaches, black bears become very fat. In a frenzy of late-summer eating, they may gain as much as 30 pounds (14 kg) a week. This is their last chance to get in shape for the winter. Just prior to denning time, the bears stop feeding, their stomachs becoming shrunken and half-rigid. In this condition, the bears retire to a cave or hollow log and become dormant. Quite often they will drag leaves and tree branches into the hole to make a cozy nest. In the Great Smoky Mountains and elsewhere in the U.S. Southeast, most bears den above ground in tree cavities formed in wind-damaged hardwood trees. Sleeping chambers are enlarged by scraping the cavity walls; the punky wood chips are then used as bedding material.

A study conducted by Michael Pelton, a University of Tennessee bear-biologist, showed that the smaller size of female black bears allows them to use dens that have entrances too small for marauding male bears to enter. This protects the cubs from harm and reinforces, incidentally, the selective advantage of small female body size.

Black bears in northern Canada den earlier and remain in their dens much longer than do those in the south. After the first frost of September they seek out their den sites and are usually in hibernation by October. They emerge from their dens in late April, looking gaunt after their long fast. In Idaho, black bears dig their dens in October and enter in early November, remaining there until mid-April. In Florida, and probably in other southeastern states, most black bears, except pregnant females, remain active through the winter. (A northern bear

Snug in its hollow-tree den, this hibernating black bear sleepily eyes the photographer. Some bears seem to be easier to wake than others. (Dennis McAllister)

that does not have sufficient fat for hibernating may also be active all winter.)

Body temperatures of hibernating black bears range from 91.4° F to 99.4° F (33° to 37.4° C). Black bear blood has more, but smaller, circulating red blood cells than do humans or dogs. This condition appears to be an advantage to a hibernating species because it increases the surface area of its red corpuscles. This in turn provides a more efficient exchange of oxygen and carbon dioxide.

Spring is a negative forage time for hibernating bears; they usually continue to lose weight for a couple of months after leaving the dens, or just maintain it if they're lucky. By the time summer's abundance arrives, life has become a nonstop effort to eat and gain weight.

MANAGING A COMEBACK

Heavily hunted during the settlement of eastern North America, black bears were gunned down by the thousands for meat, fat, and fur. Huge expanses of forest habitat were cleared for farming. The bears became very scarce; what was left of the population withdrew, finding sanctuary in the few undeveloped places. Today, the black bear of the East is found in isolated pockets between cities and major agricultural areas. Wildlife agencies, concerned by the disappearance of the bear, began campaigns for the bears' conservation in the 1940s.

Efforts at black-bear management in the region are paying off; there are many more black bears now than there were fifty years ago. In Pennsylvania, the bear population has doubled since the 1970s, to about 7,000. New York, with a human population of about 20 million, also has about 4,100 black bears.

The Urbanized Bears of New Jersey

By the mid-1900s, the number of bears in New Jersey had fallen to just twenty. Hunting was finally stopped in 1971, and by 1986 the population had risen to nearly sixty. Patricia McConnell, black-bear manager for the N.J. Department of Environmental Protection, describes the state's current bear situation:

> Our bears have become very cosmopolitan—they really have no other choice—because the majority of our sightings are in people's backyards. Most of the residents are surprised, though tolerant . . . others are so delighted at seeing bears that they begin the undesirable habit of feeding them. One of these bears has become so acclimated to being fed that he often visits other houses and stares into their picture windows. He sits for hours, often drooling in anticipation of being fed, prompting many calls to the police about a possible "rabid bear." These incidents are just thirty-six miles from Manhattan.

I heard a rumor that Patricia McConnell knows every bear in New Jersey by name. One day, one of "her" bears came into the town of North Haledon, only fifteen miles from New York City. He was seen wandering through people's yards and down the streets. Following McConnell's recommendations, the police left him alone and he eventually found his way out of the city. Earlier, near Trenton, the state's capital, a black bear (followed by over 100 people and a helicopter) ran through the middle of a Fish, Game and Wildlife Department employees' baseball game. Everyone had a good time.

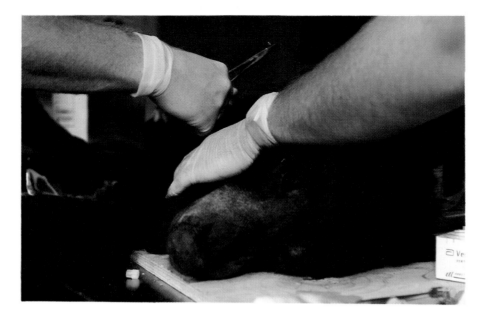

Under anesthesia, the injured bear lies quietly as its wounds are sutured. In a few days it will be released back into the wild. This pioneering veterinary team has provided emergency medical help to hundreds of injured bears and other wildlife in the park.

Across the western part of the continent, black bears have done fairly well during the past 100 years of "progress." Black bear densities are quite high in most areas. In the state of Washington, various estimates by different "bear people" place the state's population somewhere between 30,000 and 60,000 bears. These high numbers allow the Fish and Game Department to run a liberal autumn bear-hunting season. In western Washington there is an additional spring hunting season aimed at decreasing the number of timber trees killed by bears.

Mr. Flowers and the Tree-Peeling Bears

The coastal timber districts of northern California, Oregon, Washington, and southern British Columbia have exceptionally high bear populations. For the most part, these bears cause very few problems, except in spring. For some reason, especially during the months of May and June, bears crave the inner, juicy cambium layers of prized timber trees such as Douglas fir. To get at the cambium, bears strip the bark from trees, girdling and killing them. To the timber industry, this is a serious problem. Over the years, millions of dollars of timber have been lost because of bear damage. One hungry bear can peel fifty trees in a night and do $20,000 damage over the spring. In some areas, over half the harvestable trees are destroyed.

The problem became apparent in 1940, and it increased to the point that it was obvious to the timber industry that something had to be done. This is when the Washington Forest Protection Association (WFPA), a forest industry cooperative, hired seven professional hunters to take unlimited numbers of bears. On the Olympic Peninsula alone, two people hunting in the same area took a total of nearly 300 bears each summer. One of those hunters was a man named Ralph Flowers, from Aberdeen, Washington. Mr. Flowers explains what happened:

> This killing activity was kept up through the 1960s when we completed a bear research program to try and find out why bears peel trees and what could be done to control the problem besides killing them. After a quarter of a million dollars and three years, we had determined that the cambium layer of the tree was a sort of emergency food supply in the spring. But we still didn't have any real answer to how to prevent them from peeling trees.

Efforts by the Washington State Fish and Game Department to find a solution had failed, and research by the agency was dropped. The WFPA retained

Dubbed the bear "mash unit," a team of rangers and medical technicians cooperate to save the life of a black bear that has been hit by a automobile in Great Smokies National Park.

Ralph Flowers weighs a bucket of food pellets during his experiments with supplemental feeding of wild black bears in the early spring as a method of controlling timber damage.

Ralph Flowers refills a supplemental food bucket that has been emptied by hungry bears; he has determined that tree damage by bears has dropped significantly in his control areas.

Its bark peeled and girdled by a foraging black bear, this conifer on Washington's Olympic Peninsula will soon die. Forest plantations in this district often lose hundreds of trees to bear damage each year.

Ralph Flowers and some of the other hunters to continue tracking down and eliminating problem bears. This was something they had become very good at; it is now estimated that less than 20 percent of the original bear population remains in these control areas. But the hunters did not eliminate the problem. The remaining bears still peel trees in the spring.

For over thirty-eight years, Ralph Flowers killed bears for a livelihood. His total kill, over 1,125 bears, quite possibly may be more than any other living person's. Some of his close contacts with bears are recorded in scars. Gray hair hides a line of stitches that put back his scalp after a bear roughed him up. Lumps left by a bear's pointed teeth misshape his left arm and speckle his right hand where he was bitten. His trigger finger is stiff and will no longer close.

Ralph Flowers still works for the WFPA, but his heart is no longer in the work of killing. Oddly enough, he may become the unlikely benefactor of the bears he has hunted for so long. He is now conducting an experiment that may stop the slaughter.

''The bears do most of the damage during the first four or five weeks after emergence from hibernation,'' says Mr. Flowers. ''That's when the bears are the hungriest and have the least amount of food available to them. So, instead of hunting them, I wondered what would happen if I fed them during that critical time.''

Ralph Flowers concocted an inexpensive food supplement made from fruit pulp and other ingredients. He then convinced one timber company to at least give the idea a try. In 1985 he set up feeding stations near damaged trees in a 75-square-mile test area. The bears ate the food and liked it so much that further timber damage stopped in that area. The cost of the food for the first experiment came to less than $50 per bear. According to Ralph Flower's figures, it currently costs more than $600 to track and kill each tree-peeling nuisance bear.

The Washington State Department of Fish and Game officially recognized Ralph Flower's idea and commissioned him to test his feeders in a much larger area of forest, starting in 1986. If his efforts are successful, then professional bear hunting will be stopped and the spring bear hunt eliminated. His latest report looks very encouraging. Says Mr. Flowers:

> The third-year feeders showed improvement in damage levels . . . almost to 100 percent. I feel this improvement is attributable to two factors. The first being that bears introduced to supplemental feeding in 1985 sought out these same feeder locations . . . the second factor . . . was the overwhelming acceptance of the new pellet formula that resulted in an elevenfold increase in pellet consumption. . . . It is hoped that as more and more female bears introduce their offspring to a May–June diet of food pellets, there will be less and less instruction in tree-peeling for the young.

Ralph Flowers's experiment may soon result in changes in bear-hunting practices in other states where tree damage is also a problem. Even if the cost of feeding becomes more expensive and equals the cost of killing, it is still preferable, because, as Mr. Flowers puts it, "You've still got the bear, you've still got the trees, and the public is happier with you."

An alert black bear sniffs the air for clues to a possible meal. Prowling along the river, the bear may discover a dead fish, some succulent berries, or even a patch of tender grasses to include in its daily diet.

BROWN BEARS:

Lords of the Mountains

The brown bear *(Ursus arctos)* has the widest distribution of all bears in the world. Its range includes much of the Northern Hemisphere, from the edges of the arctic seas of North America, Europe, and Asia, south over tundra-covered mountains, across the boreal forests of Canada and the Soviet Union, down as far as Mexico, Spain, and Iran. On both continents, the southern edges of its range are marked by widely scattered, isolated populations. Although brown bears may be found in a variety of habitats, they generally prefer regions punctuated by river valleys, mountain forests, and open meadows.

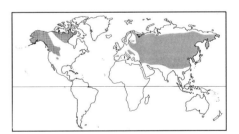

THE BROWN BEAR'S BODY

The brown bear is stout and rather chunky in shape, with a large hump of fat and muscle over the shoulders and very long claws. It has a wide, massive head that some people describe as being somewhat "dish faced" in appearance. That big head is equipped with extremely powerful jaws. I once saw a big male, trapped in a leg snare set by researchers, take out its frustration on some neighboring trees. In one bite he bit completely through a 4-inch (10-cm) -diameter pine, snapping it off. It also chewed through several 6- and 8-inch (15- and 20-cm) -diameter trees. One stump looked as though it had been dynamited. When we slammed the sharp end of a geologist's pick into the trunk of one of those trees, it only penetrated about 1.5 inches (3.8 cm) into the wood.

At Alaska's Brooks Falls, a brown bear tries to interrupt the upstream spawning migration of a sockeye salmon. During the peak of the run, this bear will live almost exclusively on fish.

A Bear With Too Many Names

A brown bear's fur is shaggy and comes in many colors—black, cinnamon, red, blond, or a mixture of these colors. In fact, this species is so variable in size and coloration that it confused the late nineteenth-century naturalists who described them. Many of these biologists thought each variation was a new species, and the resulting list of new bear "species" became so lengthy that nearly every mountain range could claim to have its own species of brown bear.

The work of Dr. C. Hart Merriam, who was an authority on brown bears, typifies what happened. In 1918 he described no fewer than eighty-six species and subspecies of brown/grizzly bears for North America, one-third of them in Alaska. Merriam lived in the age of "splitters," when minor variations in skull, size, hair color, and other differences were used to describe a new species. Had he been classifying people, I wonder how many species of humans he would have come up with. Scientists are now going the other way, generally lumping the highly variable brown bear into just one species, *Ursus arctos*. Nine or ten

Brown bears are large animals with extremely flexible forepaws and powerful jaws.

Ravaged by an angry brown bear that had been live-trapped in a foot snare, this tree stump looks almost as if it has been dynamited.

Captured by a cable snare around its forelimb, a Montana grizzly roars out its frustration.

subspecies are still recognized and argued about, but most of the confusion has been weeded out.

Some biologists believe the highly adaptable brown bear is intelligent enough to be ranked with primates, like monkeys and baboons. Many survival skills are passed on from mother to cub. Their hulking, loose-skinned shape also hides a remarkable agility that allows them to sprint up to 35 miles an hour (56 kmph) to catch a salmon in their teeth. Brown bears have good hearing and eyesight (probably equal to our own) and a sense of smell rivaling a bloodhound's.

BROWN BEAR FOOD STRATEGIES

Practically anything edible is grist to the brown bear's mill. To fuel such a large body, the bears must consume a lot of calories—up to 80 or 90 pounds (36 to

The moment of truth has arrived for a salmon trying to leap the falls.

41 kg) of food a day during the peak of the season. By eating this much food, a big bear can gain from 3 to 6 pounds (1.25 to 2.75 kg) of fat in a 24-hour period. Physiologically, they are driven to gain at this rapid rate, because the time of summer abundance is very short and the winters are long.

Although the mainstay of the brown bear's diet is mostly plant material, they eagerly seek out animal matter because its food value is much more concentrated. Whatever the bears are eating at any given time of the year, you can bet they are consuming the most nutritional foods available. In Alaska I have watched brown bears placidly grazing on sedge grasses (*Carex* species) out on the tidal flats. When seen from a distance, they could have easily been mistaken for cattle. Chemical analysis of these plants have shown that they can exceed 25 percent protein content during late June and early July. Usually this is just before the big salmon runs occur.

These huge upriver pulses of spawning fish represent an unparalleled opportunity, not only for the bears, but for a host of smaller scavengers who clean up the leftovers. Gulls hang about, waiting for scraps. Skulking foxes search for discarded fish. In this time of overabundance there is plenty of fish for nearly any appetite.

Belly Flops and Other Fishing Techniques

In fishing, each bear uses its own individual style. Some plunge headlong into the river and grab the fish in their jaws. Others wait quietly for a salmon to come by and then quickly pin it with a forepaw. Sometimes the techniques are funny. One young and obviously inexperienced bear at Mikfik Creek, in south-western Alaska, would throw himself into a pool of fish with a resounding belly flop. It was great theater, but the method didn't catch many salmon. Another bear, this one a female at Katmai's Brooks Falls, would stand at the one place where the salmon are able to jump high enough to clear the obstructing rocks and would snap them out of the air. A huge old male at the same falls would climb into the plunge pool below the rocks and stretch his forelimbs out into the current. When a salmon brushed one of them, he would quickly pin it with the opposite paw. Unlike the popular image many people have of fishing bears, I have never seen one flip a fish out of the water with its paw.

To me, the bears' most fascinating fishing technique is a behavior called "snorkeling." While holding its breath, a bear will push its head underwater while wading up the river or through a pool. When a snorkeling bear sees a fish nearby, he rushes it with open jaws.

Bears don't like to get their ears wet, though. I have seen them often, cruising through quiet water like some furry submarine, with only their ears protruding above the surface. When a bear comes up with a fish in its mouth, the first thing it will do is to shake its head in order to clear its ears. Perhaps waterlogged ears reduce the bear's ability to detect intruders.

Most bears spend a great deal of time evaluating and avoiding the threat posed by the presence of other bears near a salmon stream. But accidental encounters do occur; I once saw two intently snorkeling bears bump into each other, nose to nose. What a surprise it was to everyone! I had never heard a bear roar underwater before.

When salmon are especially numerous, brown bears will often eat just their favorite portions of the fish. I have seen bears catch, partly eat, and discard up to twenty salmon in an hour. First, they would bite into the head, eating the

Heading ashore for a leisurely meal, this Alaskan brown bear may eat a dozen or more large salmon in a single afternoon.

brain. Next, if the fish was a female, they would consume the eggs, and then peel and eat the skin. The discarded carcasses never go to waste. Usually they are claimed by some subadult bear who is not yet big enough to claim fishing rights. The bears nearly always leave the stomach, intestinal tract, and liver to the gulls and foxes.

Other Foods

Where brown bears do not have access to salmon, they will eat spawning trout and other fish. Bears with access to the seashore will scrounge through the beach drift, eating seaweed, mollusks, crabs, and washed-up bodies of sea mammals. Inland brown bears will eat moose calves, deer, elk, and caribou. The remains of a carcass too big to consume in a single meal may be buried and carefully guarded for future meals. In Japan, the brown bear's primary food source is plants: hog's fennel, acorns, fruits, and berries. A study of their scats (feces) showed that 98.7 percent of their fare was of plant origin. This diet is supplemented by licking up the winged insects that concentrate under flat rocks on lake shores and, occasionally, by eating domestic livestock.

Right: A successful bear enjoys its favorite part of a salmon—the skin.

Taken with a submersible robot camera, this photo shows a salmon's-eye view of a snorkeling bear.

Right: Having stripped the salmon of its fat-rich skin, the bear carries the rest of the fish ashore.

Below: Snorkeling for salmon in a quiet river pool, a brown bear is careful not to get its ears wet.

Top far right: Shaking like an overgrown dog, a brown bear dries its coat after a swim.

Bottom far right: Watching for possible scraps, a flock of hopeful seagulls crowds around a feeding bear.

Nuzzling the first autumn snow, this bear will soon be hibernating in its den.

Brown Bear Hibernation

In all parts of their range, except perhaps in eastern Turkey and Iran, brown bears spend the winter months hibernating in dens. At the beginning of the denning season, they may have 6 to 10 inches (15 to 25 cm) of fat under their skin. Den sites are usually remote, isolated from human activity and development. Noise from machinery and aircraft is disturbing and may force some bears to avoid the area for future denning. In the Soviet Union, brown bears that have not found a denning site are considered particularly dangerous.

Rock caves and hollows excavated under large trees or dug horizontally into hillsides are the commonest types of dens. Often they contain a short tunnel leading to the sleeping chamber. Depending upon the size of the bear, a sleeping chamber can measure over 7 feet wide and 3 feet high (2 m by 1 m). Some dens have been used for centuries by numerous generations of bears.

In the more northern parts of their range, brown bears will sometimes den as early as the middle of September. Farther south, denning may be as late as October or November. When the bears emerge in April or May, they head for the nearest place where they might expect to find food.

A convenient rock serves as a chair for a brown bear resting after an energetic afternoon fishing for salmon.

Above: A close bond is formed between a mother bear and her cubs.

Top right: Eyes wide with consternation, three baby brown bears go for their first swim.

Bottom right: Reclining on a comfortable bed of grass, a mother pauses to nurse her half-grown cubs.

BROWN BEAR REPRODUCTION

Brown bears may live longer than thirty years and can reproduce for most of their lives. One female kept at the Leipzig Zoo was still having cubs when she was twenty-six years old. Females generally don't breed until they are least five years old. The breeding season usually occurs in June or July. On Hokkaido Island in Japan, brown bears give birth about 222 to 229 days after copulation. However, because of delayed implantation, the actual fetal growth takes only about sixty days. (A one-month-old embryo is about the size of a mouse.) Nearly naked and helpless, the cubs are born in the winter den in January, February, or March. The average litter size is two, but as many as four young are not uncommon, especially in regions where food is abundant.

A newborn brown bear may weigh less than 1 pound (.45 kg), but nursing cubs gain weight quickly because bear milk contains as much as 33 percent fat. As they grow up, the cubs may increase their weight as much as 1,000 times.

A deep bond unites the mother with her cubs, and she will fiercely defend them from potential harm. But many cubs are still lost (some 10 to 40 percent), especially during their first one and a half years of life. Their deaths are frequently due to encounters with adult males; sometimes the mother is also killed by these marauding bears. Wolves also sometimes prey on young brown bear cubs.

The cubs den with their mother for two winters and then are chased off in the spring when she goes into estrus again. Every third year she may produce another set of cubs. If for some reason the mother does not mate, the family may den together again for a third winter. After family separation, the young males move out of their mother's home range; subadult females tend to remain.

Social groups that include several females and all their offspring are occasionally reported. Larry Aumiller, a biologist at the McNeil River Sanctuary, observed one of these groups during the course of one of his summers there:

> The two females had eight cubs between them. All through the summer, first one would lead the cubs and then they would switch . . . and the other would have the cubs. I took several photos that showed one of the mothers nursing six cubs. The next day she had only two. These two mothers were good, tolerant females . . . bears that had known each other for a number of years. When they would come together, the cubs would scatter every which way. Then one mother would leave with six and the other would have only one.

It seems brown bears are more social than we might think.

Full of energy, even when relaxing, a young bear plays footsie with a stick.

THE GIANT BEARS OF KAMCHATKA

The rugged Kamchatka Peninsula is a great finger of land jutting south from eastern Russia into the sea north of Japan. The majority of Kamchatkan bears are relatively small animals, comparable to those of northern Europe. But native legends tell of a giant race of black-colored bears, some of which weigh more than 2,500 pounds (1,134 kg). The first scientific evidence that brown bears this size might really exist was presented during the 1950s in a report about the investigations of Dr. Stan Bergman of the State Museum of Natural History at Stockholm, who spent two years on the Kamchatka Peninsula. Apparently the bears were either too hard to approach or very scarce because Dr. Bergman never saw a living specimen. He was, however, able to photograph a bear's footprints in the snow. It left a track 15 inches (38 cm) long and 10 inches (25 cm) wide. Later, Dr. Bergman was shown the largest bearskin he had ever seen. It was covered with short hair, in contrast to the long hair of other Kamchatkan bears. He also measured a gigantic bear skull. Based on his measurements, this bear would have been much bigger than the largest known Kodiak bears living just across the Bering Strait.

The wildness of the country and its dense vegetation help to protect Kamchatka bears from probing scientists and hunters. Because certain key Soviet military bases are located on Kamchatka, most of the area is closed to foreign visitors and to many Russian citizens. However, a few Soviet officials are allowed to hunt in the region during special vacations. One high-ranking official, who later defected to the United States, told me about his hunt for bears on the peninsula. He never got to shoot the giant black-colored bear, but he said he had heard that several monster-sized bears were living in the vicinity where the hunt took place. There is a very good possibility that these bears are a local variant of the Siberian brown bear *(Ursus arctos beringianus)*, which lives on the surrounding mainland and is said to attain very large sizes, to 1,800 pounds (816 kg).

If the giant bear does exist, Soviet biologists haven't mentioned it. I suppose we will just have to wait until the Soviet's security regulations are relaxed before we will know for sure if this giant-sized bear, said to feast on salmon, really is found in the dense thickets along Kamchatka's rivers—or only in the imaginations of local residents.

OTHER ASIAN BROWN BEARS

In the northern mountains of India and in other parts of the Himalayas lives a reddish-colored brown bear very similar in appearance to the American grizzly. It also has those white-colored hair tips that give the coat its grizzled, silvery tinge. Called the red bear *(Ursus arctos isabellinus)* by the people of the region, it is about the size of a large grizzly, ranging from 5.5 to 8 feet (1.7 to 2.5 m) in length. Red bears that live above the tree line feed on grasses, roots, and the occasional ibex killed in an avalanche. Herdsmen shoot the mothers and capture the cubs, which are then sold to gypsies and other itinerant entertainers for use as dancing bears.

Other races of Asian brown bears include the little-known Manchurian brown bear *(Ursus arctos manchuricus)* and the so-called horse bear *(Ursus arctos pruinosus)* of Tibet, Sichuan, and other western provinces of China. This bear is often bicolored, with a yellow-brown or whitish cape forming a saddle-shaped marking across its shoulders. Horse bears are very much feared in the regions where they are found. While photographer Mark Newman and I were traveling through China seeking information about bears, a biologist with considerable experience with bears told us that nearly 1,500 people are killed by horse bears each year. At first, this number seemed fantastic. But apparently, most of the mauling victims are farmers who live in the mountains flanking the Tibetan Plateau. There is a great push now to clear new ground and expand the area under cultivation on each farm. When a conflict over territorial rights begins with one of these big brown bears, the farmer usually loses. Guns are not generally allowed in the country, so most people are armed with just shovels and hoes, which are next to useless as weapons against an enraged bear. But as progress pushes inexorably forward, the bears will soon become the losers.

HIGUMA, THE BROWN BEAR OF JAPAN

Japan is a small place full of big surprises. In this crowded country of nearly 122 million people, enough wildland remains to support nearly 3,000 brown bears and an unestimated number of Asian black bears. The brown bears are found only on Hokkaido, Japan's northernmost island. But this island of a little more than 30,000 square miles (77,000 sq km) has nearly four times the brown bear population of the entire continental United States!

About 150 years ago the Japanese introduced agriculture and industry to Hokkaido and began to clear the land. For 1,000 years or more the aboriginal Ainu had lived here by hunting bears and deer, catching salmon, and gathering plants. To kill these big bears without guns, the Ainu used bamboo arrows poisoned with a preparation made from the roots of a small purple-flowered plant called *Aconitum yesoense*. Hunters would test the strength of the poison by putting a bit on the tongue or the web between the fingers. If there was a burning sensation, then the poison was strong enough. After being hit, the bear would run only about 50 to 100 yards (50 to 100 m) before collapsing from the fast-acting poison.

Each Ainu village periodically gave thanks to the bear during a remarkable winter festival featuring the killing and eating of a captured bear cub that had been raised for about two years in the village. (When the bear was a small cub, the village women would even taken turns nursing it from their own breasts.) The four-day-long ceremony was supposed to send the bear back to the mountain gods as an honored messenger of the village.

The Japanese government forbade the Ainu festival some twenty-five years ago. Now only a mock festival, held for tourists, prevents the old ways from becoming entirely lost. Noako Maeda, curator at the Noboribetsu Bear Park, in Noboribetsu, Japan, is deeply interested in anything having to do with the bears of Hokkaido. She has studied the ways of the Ainu and has even nursed young cubs. (She says they suckle very gently, more so than her own children.) Noako Maeda hopes to see surplus bears raised at the park eventually released into the wild.

However, these good intentions may never be realized because most Japanese people consider the brown bear a dangerous pest. The bears regularly kill and eat livestock and sometimes even kill mushroom pickers or fisherfolk in the mountains. *Higuma,* the local name for this bear, has traditionally been an animal with a price on its head. In 1915, a bear attacked a farming settlement, killing eight people, including a baby. Bounties of 10,000 to 20,000 yen are still offered by some communities. Each year some 300 to 400 bears are killed as nuisances.

The future for *higuma* doesn't warrant much optimism. Their habitat is steadily diminishing as the natural forests are cut and as new farms and residences are built. Most of the rivers that have salmon in them are now under human control and closed to the bears. Concern for the bears' dilemma of shortage of living space and food has recently prompted the formation of a research group based at Hokkaido University in Sapporo. Officials at the university still officially adhere to the government's view of the bears as pests and so do not officially recognize the research group. Unofficially, the group is tolerated and even allowed to use volunteer help in its programs. For the last several years these dedicated students have been studying how *higuma* subsists. Perhaps they will discover a way to protect people's lives and property and at the same time save Japan's big bears.

THE RENAISSANCE OF EUROPEAN BEARS

In Europe, brown bears developed their own strategy for surviving around civilization. Centuries of constant hunting severely decimated their numbers. In Britain, they survived up to the Middle Ages. In most other European countries, brown bear populations were reduced to remnant levels by the middle of the nineteenth century. The bears had been practically wiped out by the end of World War II. Very few sanctuaries existed where the big bear could live without encountering people. The bears that did survive became very secretive and extremely clever at concealing themselves from people.

In Norway, scientists discovered seventeen separate populations of brown bears that had managed to escape notice. In the Brenta area of northern Italy, bears had become so scarce that local people assumed they were extinct. The occasional hunter's story of seeing bear prints was openly scoffed at. Eventually,

however, a Swiss researcher named Hans Roth managed to trap two of the wary animals and fit them with radio transmitters. By doggedly tracking them with a directional radio receiver, he finally learned these bears' way of life. He discovered that nearly every aspect of their behavior is characterized by an attempt to avoid humans. They spend each day hidden in a different location, seldom leave the woods, and forage for food only at night. Much to the amazement of the people of Brenta, some fifteen to eighteen bears still live in the area today.

Europe is experiencing a renaissance in the rediscovery and management of its brown bears. About 20 bears have been found living in the Spanish and French Pyrénées. Norway now has about 200 bears, and the population is slowly increasing. Sweden allows controlled hunting of its approximately 600 bears in an attempt to kill those bears that feed heavily on domestic livestock; the bear damage, totaling about 100 head of sheep each year, is reimbursed by the state. Norway and Czechoslovakia also have government compensation programs. Yugoslavian bears are not yet protected by law, but by agreement among hunting associations, and the country's current bear population is about 300 animals. An artificially high population of bears is maintained by a supplemental feeding program on Yugoslavia's Koprivnica Hunting Preserve near the town of Bugojno; each year over 200 tons of corn and 500 tons of slaughterhouse refuse are fed to the preserve's 150 bears.

Rumania has more bears than any other country in central Europe. Because of state protection and limited shooting, their numbers have risen from about 1,000 animals in 1940, to nearly 4,000 today. In an area called the Soviet Karelia, located in Russia's northwest corner, there are presently about 3,000 bears.

Forced to sneak through the back-yards of civilization, the European brown bear's very existence often seems to be characterized by caution.

Here, the species has reached the saturation point for its habitat, and surplus bears are migrating westward into Finland, where bears live in smaller densities. (The Finnish bear population is estimated to be about 400 animals.) In the Soviet Carpathians, brown bears damage up to 50 percent of the timber trees in some districts, especially spruces and larches. Management there is not aimed at eliminating the bear, but rather at reducing the damage. In France, there is even a project to reintroduce the brown bear into the Alps. The last bear was killed there in 1934.

Some scientists believe the biggest problem now facing the continued survival of Europe's brown bears is genetic deterioration caused by inbreeding. To expand the gene pool, a few researchers are attempting to augment some small, isolated populations by introducing surplus bears trapped in other areas.

Until the turn of the century brown bears lived in the Atlas Mountains of northern Africa. They were probably hunted out by the Moors. A few relic populations of brown bears may still exist in isolated areas northeast of the Mediterranean Sea.

RACES OF NORTH AMERICAN BROWN BEARS

Ninty percent of North America's estimated 40,000 to 50,000 brown bears are found in Alaska, the Yukon, the Rocky Mountains of Alberta and British Columbia, and in the mainland Northwest Territories. Less than 800 bears still exist in the continental United States. These bears have long been the subject of bitter political infighting on just how to manage their continued existence. Lawmakers have even gone so far as to classify the grizzly as an endangered species in their attempts to make federal and state funds available for research and conservation projects. On the rest of the continent, and throughout the world, the bear seems to be doing very well and is in no danger of extinction.

At present only two subspecies of brown bears are thought to occur on the North American continent. One is the grizzly *(Ursus arctos horribilis)*, a race of brown bear living in the interior forests of North America. The term "grizzly" is a colloquial name that refers to the animal's coloration. It usually has a dark coat with shimmering silvery-tipped hairs that give it a "grizzled" appearance, at least when viewed from a distance. Weights of most adult grizzlies range from 350 to 700 pounds (158 to 317 kg), rarely going over 1,000 pounds (453 kg). In the mountains of northern Canada, where winters are long and cold and the forage is sparse, the heaviest male recorded in a five-year study weighed only 471 pounds (214 kg). Females are smaller than males and do not continue to gain weight with age as males do.

The grizzly's reputation for ferociousness toward people makes the animal seem much larger. Though not always undeserved, these horror stories have hampered the public's understanding of this generally shy and peaceful animal. As one biologist put it, "This is an emotional species." Every year a half dozen people get mauled by grizzlies, further reinforcing public attitudes. These incidents were usually precipitated by the victim's lack of knowledge about bears.

GLACIERS GROW BIG BEARS

In the coastal areas of Alaska and British Columbia live the largest brown bears found on the North American continent. Their huge size seems to be a result of a tremendous productivity associated with the active glaciers of the region. Glacial movements grind the surrounding rocks into powder, making its mineral nutrients available to a great variety of food plants. It is also theorized that when these nutrients are washed into rivers and down to the sea they stimulate a heavy plankton bloom, which in turn feeds a large fish population throughout the region. The bears then harvest some of this abundance when it returns to the rivers in the form of salmon.

In southwestern Alaska, three major sanctuaries have been established in order to protect these bears and their habitat.

The Kodiak National Wildlife Refuge

Kodiak is a ruggedly beautiful island off Alaska's southwestern coast, dotted with human settlements and ranches. In 1941, over half of this 5,300-square-mile (13,700 sq km) chunk of land, along with portions of nearby Afognak and Shuyak islands, was set aside to protect the habitat of brown bears and other wildlife. The region is characterized by mountains accented with fjordlike inlets, meadows, lush vegetation, and wet, stormy weather.

The Kodiak brown bear *(Ursus arctos middendorffi)*, lives isolated from its brethren on a few islands in Alaska's Kodiak island group. Kodiak bears are often thought to be the largest brown bears in the world. An adult male Kodiak bear might weight 1,800 pounds (816 kg).

An estimated 2,500 to 3,000 Kodiak brown bears live in this northern archipelago. About 10,000 years ago they were isolated from the rest of the world when a glacier cut off the area from the mainland. Since then, Kodiak's bears have been slowly evolving away from the rest of their Alaskan cousins. Today, they are generally larger—a big male may weigh 1,500 pounds (680 kg)—and have wider faces and a more inflated cranium. On the basis of these skull differences, most scientists categorize the Kodiak bear as a distinct subspecies.

Fifty years ago, Kodiak's bears were heading down the extermination trail. Ranchers had introduced cattle to the island, and the bears found them easy prey. The ranchers complained, and the government sent in professional hunters to kill the bears. Today, ranchers still occasionally lose cattle to the bears, but the economic loss is insignificant compared to the tourist value of the bears. Limited hunting is allowed on the refuge, and about 130 bears are shot each year. Some recent studies indicate that an individual Kodiak brown bear is worth more than $10,000 (US) in business for Kodiak's guide services, air charter companies, restaurants, and motels. If well managed, this resource should continue to provide the communities of Kodiak with needed income. There is also evidence that the limited hunting is actually increasing the bear population by eliminating some of the big males that kill cubs.

McNeil River Sanctuary

About 140 miles (225 km) north of Kodiak island and about 200 air miles (321 km) southwest of Anchorage is a medium-sized river that drains into Kamishak Bay under the shadow of an active volcano on Augustine Island. Each summer the river becomes a focal point for migrating salmon heading for their spawning grounds upstream—and for the brown bears that eat them. At one spot in the river, a series of cascades restricts the movement of the fish, forcing them to school up and splash their way over the rushing, shallow water. It is here, at this natural bottleneck, where the world's largest concentration of wild brown bears gathers to feed. Up to fifty-six bears have been seen at the falls at one time.

Realizing its uniqueness, the state of Alaska outlawed hunting in the area, and in 1976, designated some 85,000 acres (34,400 ha) along the river as a sanctuary. Over years of exposure to visitors, the bears at McNeil River have developed a remarkable tolerance toward humans. In order to minimize the impact on the bear's natural behavior, however, sanctuary managers allow only a limited number of people to visit the area. Each year about 200 applicants are picked by lottery to go, 10 at a time. Resident biologists act as guides and interpreters. When their four-day permit expires, another group flies in. By conducting their activities in a predictable and unobtrusive manner, visitors can safely witness an array of natural bear behavior and interactions at close range. Many experienced naturalists and wildlife photographers rank McNeil River Reserve as one of the best wildlife-viewing opportunities in the world.

Maintaining dominance over its fishing spot, a large brown bear charges a smaller and less experienced trespasser.

Katmai National Park

A few miles west of McNeil River lies Katmai National Park and Monument. Originally Katmai was set aside as a natural volcanic area, but over the years it has gained considerable attention as an important bear sanctuary. As many as 600 brown bears roam the park. When I spent part of a summer there I was amazed at the numbers of bears that passed by my tent on their way to the river. At nearby Brooks Falls, an elevated viewing platform allows visitors to safely watch them fish.

During mid-July a massive sockeye salmon run occurs in the Brooks River, attracting bears from the surrounding countryside. Visitors to the park headquarters at Brooks Camp are greeted by a ranger who discusses the park's safety regulations. Here, the bears have the right-of-way at all times. Camping is permitted as long as all food and garbage is carefully stored in the elevated caches the park service has built.

Katmai rangers constantly monitor the bears in the vicinity of Brooks Camp. If one starts behaving aggressively toward people, they teach it a little respect by peppering its rump with rubber bullets. Only one person has ever been injured by a bear there: A sleeping camper with bacon grease on his pants got nipped on the butt.

Brown bears also occur in great numbers in two other locations: Southeastern Alaska's "ABC" Islands (Admiralty, Baranof, and Chichagof) and in British

Recently on their own, two subadult Kodiak brown bears roughhouse in a meadow. Siblings may travel together for a year or more.

Serious conflicts are rare, but here three bears engage in an all-out argument over right-of-way. Such actions usually result in the losers running away with only a few bites and cuts to nurse. But sometimes an adult bear may be killed.

Columbia's Khutzeymateen valley. Because of concern over the negative impact of industrial logging, portions of these areas are also beginning to be managed as bear sanctuaries.

Blanche: A Grizzly's Story

Canadian wildlife-biologist Bruce McLellan calls his work "cowboy biology." He rides herd over a population of inland brown bears living in the upper Flathead River Valley of Montana and British Columbia. In the autumn, McLellan live-traps bears with leg snares and attaches radio-transmitting collars around their necks after first knocking them out with tranquilizer darts. Then, for the rest of the year, he monitors them to learn their movements and denning sites. The project, called the Border Grizzly Project, is a long-term cooperative research effort between the United States and Canada.

One of the project's goals is to determine the effects on the bears of commercial logging operations and mineral exploration. Although few people live in the valley, the area is crisscrossed with hundreds of miles of gravel roads.

"Studying them is often an exercise in frustration," Bruce McLellan told me during a recent visit.

But there's something about the grizzly's physical mystique, their power and air of dominance, that makes me really respect them. They're intelligent too; let me tell you about Blanche.

We caught her in fall of 1979, at night, 50 feet [15 m] from our cabin door. She was crazy and very aggressive . . . she kept charging and tearing up the ground and roaring because she had hurt her foot in the snare. She was making so damn much noise that we had to drive away and camp in order to sleep. We couldn't tranquilize her in the middle of the night, it was too dark.

Since then, she has been our most productive bear as far as information is concerned. We have gotten over 600 radio locations on her, so we really got to know the old gal. Anyway, after two years or so, we decided to recapture her and change the radio collar because the battery was getting low. We tried all kinds of trap sets but she avoided them. Finally we caught her with a road-killed deer used as bait. By that time the collar was nearly three years old . . . it still worked, but the batteries were almost dead.

There she was, sitting in the trap. She hadn't even pulled the cable tight around her wrist . . . she was docile and just sat there looking at us. She had dug a hole in the ground and was sitting in it in order to protect her butt from being hit by the tranquilizing dart. She had remembered the previous capture three years ago.

So I shot the dart into her neck instead . . . the surprised look in her eyes said, "You rotten jerk . . . that's not fair!"

It's been several years since I've seen old Blanche; I wonder if she is still alive . . . she'd be over twenty-seven years old by now. . . . Yes, she was a smart one alright.

The look on this grizzled inland brown bear's face seems to be a sure warning that hell hath no fury like a mother protecting her cubs.

As we talked, Bruce steered his battered pickup truck through the bumpy maze of logging roads leading us to where he had set his snares. One by one, each trap we checked was empty. At the final snare, we stopped the truck near the end of a short spur road. While Bruce was wondering if Blanche were still alive, a movement in the direction of the set caught our attention. Leaping out of the truck, we were met by a thunderous roar that meant only one thing: Grizzly! A few moments later we discovered that it was Blanche.

After she was tranquilized, McLellan examined her. She was lactating, so she must have had cubs nearby. At twenty-seven-years old, Blanche was the oldest known grizzly to have cubs. Her teeth were worn down to nubbins.

A few months later I received a letter from Bruce:

> The fall went well with a mixture of good and bad luck. We made a total of 13 grizzly bear captures, putting out 9 new collars. Our bad luck was really Blanche's bad luck, the last she will have. The old timer was maliciously gunned down as she crossed the road. I guess some "sportsman" wanted to see if his gun really worked. It did. She was hit while on the road, made it 20 meters [22 yards] into the forest and died. She was left to the ravens. Her yearling cubs, without her guidance and care, ended up in our snares four days later, about four miles [6.5 km] from where Blanche was killed. That evening, the young bears returned to their mother's corpse . . . however, they are 150 pounds [68 kg], in good shape and will likely do fine until, like their mother, they interrupt the path of some fast-moving lead.

Looking somewhat like a storybook troll under a bridge, a Kodiak brown bear watches for the flash of a salmon or the swirling of its fins in the stream.

The Trouble with Grizzlies

"Yeah, I shoot a grizzly every couple of years or so," the cattle rancher frankly admitted to me. I had arranged to have a lunchtime meeting with him at this roadside diner in the foothills of Montana's Rocky Mountains. "Those bears are just too damned mean . . . the trouble is, they'd kill every one of my calves if they could."

He paused, swallowed a gulp of coffee, and reflected a moment. Outside stood his four-wheel drive Chevy pickup, a shotgun and a deer rifle hanging on a rack above the backrest. His ranch, what he called his "little spread up in the hills," was as big as some counties in the eastern states. He had grown up in these hills, accustomed to handling his problems by himself.

"Oh, I know the law is trying to protect them and all," he continued, "but a man's got a right to protect his property, doesn't he?"

I nodded. He had a point there. I don't think I could ignore a grizzly who turned my prized calves into mangled carcasses. However, I wondered how many of them were already dead before the bears started feeding on them.

"Well, we do get a few stillbirths and we lose a few steers now and then . . . so, maybe some of them weren't done in by the bears," he allowed. "But I sure as hell ain't taking any chances. Can't afford to . . . I'm barely able to pay our bills as it is."

We talked for over an hour, discussing bears and his outspoken politics about personal freedom. Then it was time to leave. We walked out to his truck and said our good-byes. As he swung into his pickup and headed for home, he told me once again, "Grizzlies are just too damned mean. . . . They'll get you

Still wet from the river, a mother and her cub relax on shore. Family groups sometimes stay together as long as three or four years.

if you give them half a chance. We'll never be able get along with them."

The grizzly has been at odds with civilization ever since it was first discovered by European settlers. The Lewis and Clark Expedition encountered quite a few and quickly opened fire on them. In 1848, five hunters who had spent a year in Oregon returned to the East with a total of 700 grizzly pelts. As wagon trains brought settlers toward a new life in the West, grizzlies began to fall by the thousands. By 1900, the grizzly had been eliminated from the Great Plains and surrounding hill countries. The land was beginning to be made safe for livestock. Bear skins are in great demand on the world marketplace, too. In 1904, a good brown bear pelt brought $75, equivalent to more than a month's wages. Prior to World War I, hundreds of skins were shipped to Europe for use in the dress-uniform hats of the Russian, Austrian, German, and English military.

The last grizzly in California was apparently killed in 1922. By 1933 the bear was gone from Oregon, and by 1935 it had vanished from the Southwest. Once codominant with humans, the grizzly had been reduced to a few scattered populations in the lower forty-eight states. Totaling less than 800 or 900, they still are a problem to ranchers and a menace to hikers.

In Douglas Chadwick's 1986 *National Geographic* magazine article, "Grizz: Of Men and the Great Bear," he wrote:

> Perhaps we won't lose the grizzly altogether. Perhaps we'll just change it into something else. Take a remnant population, especially a small inbreeding one. Keep blowing away the big, the bold, the conspicuous. And out of the shallow gene pool climbs a scaled-down version, meek and mild. A grizzly in name only.

Already, the grizzly is showing signs of becoming more cautious. In Yellowstone National Park, the bears are said to hide themselves and monitor the movements of humans intruding into their territory. If too many people come to the area, the bears simply leave. Where the Rocky Mountains meet the Great Plains, grizzlies are being found as far as 20 to 30 miles (32 to 48 km) out on the prairie. To get there, the bears travel along the streams that flow down from the mountains, hiding by day in the cover of thick riparian brush, to which they quickly retreat if they perceive danger while out in the open. Maybe the grizzly will indeed become retiring, like the brown bears of Europe.

A lone grizzly wanders across the expanse of an Arctic floodplain. Residents of untouched wilderness, inland brown bears often require enormous areas of land to survive.

POLAR BEARS:

Nomads of the Arctic Ice

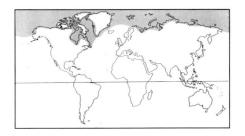

The Eskimos call him "Nanook" and credit him with supernatural powers. Little wonder, too, for this white bear that lives at the top of the world can appear out of nowhere in a land of endless ice. Polar bears differ so greatly, both in appearance and habit, from the other bears of the world that it is hard to think of them as related to brown bears. Until recently scientists even classified ice bears in a group by themselves.

EVOLUTION OF THE POLAR BEAR

Polar bears *(Ursus maritimus)* are thought to have evolved from brown bears in Siberia during the glacial advance of the mid-Pleistocene, between 250,000 and 100,000 years ago. Their habitat dissected by glaciers, the bears' ancestors were gradually pushed north onto the sea ice, where they learned to hunt seals. The harsh environment apparently stimulated rapid evolutionary changes in these isolated bears. As they became more carnivorous, their cheek teeth (carnassials) developed sharper surfaces for shearing meat into bite-sized chunks. Their long claws, previously used for digging, shortened and became needle sharp for grasping wriggling prey. The hairs of their fur became hollow and denser for protection against bitter cold, and, as camouflage in a white world, their fur became creamy white.

Though they might not look it, brown bears and polar bears are still genetically very similar. In captivity they have mated and produced fertile offspring. Some intriguing similarities are also occasionally noted in the wild. For example, brown bears in Canada's western Arctic have been observed out on the sea ice

Symbol of the Arctic, a polar bear wanders across the sunset-washed ice of a frozen sea.

and polar bears have been seen inland, hunting caribou. Some biologists think that the Barren Ground grizzly, a geographic race of brown bear living just inland from western North America's polar seas, may be a hybrid between polar bears and brown bears. Other scientists disagree, pointing out that the two species have very different habits and breeding seasons. However, the bears' breeding seasons overlap during the month of May, which would have made hybridization possible.

An extinct subspecies of polar bear, called *Ursus maritimus tyrannus*, was discovered in London in 1964. From its fossil remains, we can see that this animal was much larger than present-day polar bears.

Vital Statistics

Polar bears are among the largest members of the bear family. Females grow until they are about four years old and attain maximum weights of about 660 pounds (300 kg). Males continue to grow until about eight years of age and may weigh from 1,100 to 1,322 pounds (500 to 600 kg) and measure between 8.25 to 11.5 feet (2.5 to 3.5 m) from nose to tail. The largest recorded polar bear was a male measuring over 12 feet (3.65 m) long and weighing a reported 2,210 pounds (1,002 kg).

The polar bear's stocky body has a longer neck and proportionately smaller head than other bears'. Its powerful musculature is particularly well developed in the hind legs and neck. Its massive forepaws, up to 12 inches (30 cm) in diameter, are larger than the hind paws and are oarlike, with partially webbed toes for more efficient swimming. The soles of the feet are covered with dense pads of fur, offering better traction on ice. The bear's short tail is inconspicuous and its ears are small and furry.

An adult's stomach is very large, with a capacity for more than 150 pounds (70 kg) of food. With a digestive tract typical of carnivores, it apparently does not digest starches very well.

The polar bear's liver is extremely rich in vitamin A, ranging between 15,000 and 30,000 units per gram, which makes its liver toxic to humans. There are accounts of arctic explorers who became ill or even died from vitamin A poisoning after eating polar bear liver. As mentioned in chapter 1, polar bears are also

Right: Almost magically, a polar bear can appear out of nowhere or disappear into wind-driven snow only a few yards away.

Far right: Polar bears are among the largest members of the bear family. A polar bear's skin, as well as its nose, is black for maximum solar heat gain.

very susceptible to the parasitic worm *Trichinella*. Apparently they contract the parasite through eating infected seals, and humans can contract the parasite by eating raw or undercooked polar bear meat. Infections of trichinosis can be painful and potentially fatal, but thorough cooking of the meat to temperatures above 155° F (69° C) or freezing it for twenty-eight days in a home freezer at temperatures below 0° F (−17° C) will kill any *Trichinella* present.

THE POLAR BEAR'S COAT

Fur color varies from pure white to a yellowish hue. Sometimes, if the light conditions are right, the coat will look gray. The yellowish shade, often seen in summer, probably results from oxidation by the sun. In any event, the fur only appears white because it reflects and scatters visible light; individual hairs are clear and hollow. These hollow hairs have recently been discovered to act as a kind of ultraviolet radiation trap; they conduct it, like light within an optical fiber, to the bear's skin—which is black, as are its nose and lips. Scientists at Northeastern University in Boston have discovered that polar bear fur has an amazingly 95 percent efficiency in converting the sun's ultraviolet rays into usable heat. According to one current theory, this absorbed energy helps the animal to maintain its body temperature. Unlike solar collectors that must be aimed for maximum gain, polar bear hairs trap light coming from every direction. They lose very little of that heat because, for some reason not yet understood, the ultraviolet energy flows only toward the animal's skin.

This phenomenon was first investigated by Richard Grojean, professor of electrical and computer engineering at Northeastern University in Boston, when he became intrigued by a report made by a group of Canadian biologists who found that population estimates of polar bears could not be made by normal aerial photography or even infrared photography. Traditional aerial photography failed because polar bears blend so well into their snowy surroundings, and infrared photography, which can detect warm-blooded animals, was futile because the bear's fur is such effective insulation that almost no outside heat could be detected. The problem was finally solved by using ultraviolet photography, which registers the short, invisible rays at the far end of the light spectrum. The animals could be seen because the snow reflects 90 percent of the sun's ultraviolet rays, while polar bear fur absorbs them and provides a contrast on film.

Canadian polar-bear specialist Mitch Taylor feels that the polar bear's solar heat–collecting fur may actually have only very limited survival importance, since the coldest part of the year also has the least daylight. (Near the Arctic circle, for example, periods of winter daylight are extremely short or even nonexistent.) Citing the evidence, Taylor says:

> Yet polar bears can jump into ice water and swim fifty or sixty miles . . . there have even been reports of up to one hundred miles. What insulates the bear from excessive heat loss is its fur and a thick layer of underlying blubber. Also, a countercurrent blood system cools the blood as it goes toward the body surface and warms it as it comes back in . . . sort of an automatic heat engine, like a seal's.

The polar bear's hollow hair also increases its buoyancy when swimming. For further protection against cold, the fur is equipped with an outer layer of glossy guard hair overlying a thick and woolly layer of underhair. Some 2 to 4 inches (5 to 10 cm) of subcutaneous fat lying beneath the skin also add buoyancy and insulation.

The Swimming "Sea Bear"

Ursus maritimus means "sea bear," and this is where they are usually found—near the "active zones" where sea ice and open water mix. Polar bears are excellent swimmers and will enter the water to catch food or to escape danger. Using only their forepaws as flippers, they can swim up to 60 miles (95 km) without resting, at an average speed of about 6 miles per hour (10 kmph). The rear feet are used for steering, like rudders. The big white bears have been seen on ice floes 200 miles offshore.

Polar bears seem to enjoy swimming and are excellent divers as well. They can remain submerged for up to two minutes, as they cruise along at depths from 10 to 15 feet (3 to 4.5 m). While underwater their ears are flattened and nostrils are closed but their eyes remain open. Diving polar bears apparently can see very well while underwater; a captive specimen I worked with could spot a dead herring lying 15 feet (4.5 m) deep on the bottom of the pool. In the wild, they hunt seabirds by diving and coming up underneath them. They may also take crabs and other shellfish from the shallow seafloor.

Polar bears also use their swimming ability to hunt seals in open leads. (A lead is a long crack broken in the sea ice by wind or tidal currents; leads may remain open from only a few minutes to several days.) There are also areas that remain ice free throughout the winter called *polynyas*. These are the biologically active zones of the frozen arctic seas, and it is in these areas where the larger marine mammals such as whales and seals congregate to breathe and feed.

Sometimes a swimming polar bear will leap out of the water in order to surprise a dozing seal resting on the edge of the ice. Several accounts tell of polar bears leaping from 7 to 8 feet (2.25 m) into the air from a swimming start. They also have been observed floating motionless and gradually drifting within striking distance of a seal. When entering the water a bear may carefully slide in backwards from the edge of an ice floe or it may just leap in headfirst. When emerging from the water, the bear usually shakes itself like a wet dog.

With their remarkable undersea diving ability, polar bears have been known to bring up such edibles as seaweed, clams, crabs, and even bottom-dwelling fish.

Above: Excellent divers, polar bears can cruise to depths of fifteen feet (4.5 m) and stay submerged for more than two minutes.

Right: Polar bears seem to have excellent underwater vision and will sometimes scan the bottom of shallow bays for potential food.

Far right: Swimming seaward, a polar bear breaks through an ice crust too thin to support its weight. Occasionally, polar bears are seen swimming hundreds of miles out at sea.

Polar bears wander over vast areas of the Arctic but do not travel aimlessly. They seem to restrict their movements to specific "home" regions where they live out the course of their lives.

THE WALKING BEAR

Polar bears are great travelers, walking huge distances every year. During an average lifetime an individual bear may have traveled across 100,000 square miles (259,000 sq km) of arctic wilderness. Their normal gait is a kind of ponderous shuffle at a steady rate of about 2.5 miles an hour (4 kmph). If pressed, a polar bear can break into a run with a top speed of over 25 miles per hour (40 kmph). However, most polar bears seem to tire quickly and take the first opportunity to lie down and rest. Paul Watt, a researcher with Canada's Institute of Arctic Physiology in Churchill, Manitoba, has studied captive polar bears walking at different speeds on a treadmill and measured their oxygen consumption.

"Although polar bears have to migrate large distances, they are very inefficient walkers," he says.

> They require up to twice as much energy to walk as would be expected for other mammals their size. It's probably because of their massive legs and the whole structure of their build. Evidentally, the trade-off is to be able to have these massive forelegs in order to break through seal dens or to flip a 500-pound [227-kg] seal out of the water with one paw.

Polar bears' wide feet allow them to move through deep snow, but to save energy they prefer to travel on a solid surface such as ice or bare ground.

When descending steep hillsides, the bear may assume a semireclining position and use its extended forelegs as brakes. Polar bears have also been seen climbing steep ice cliffs and "sledding" down hills on their stomachs.

EYES, EARS, SMELL, AND INTELLIGENCE

A polar bear has excellent eyesight and hearing, at least equal to a human's. Its nose is so incredibly sensitive that it can detect a seal more than 20 miles (32 km) away. Researchers in Alaska have watched male polar bears march in a straight line, over the tops of pressure ridges of uplifted ice and through open leads, for up to 40 miles (64 km) to reach a prey animal they had detected. These bears can also sniff out seal dens covered by 3 feet (1 m) of ice and snow.

Like nearly all bears, polar bears exhibit a remarkable range of behavior. Eskimo hunters tell stories of the bears covering their dark noses with a paw or a piece of snow to keep from being seen while stalking a seal on the open ice. Other observers have seen bears use blocks of ice to break into seal igloos to get at the seal pups. Dr. Charles Jonkel, who did considerable work with polar bears in Manitoba, once saw a polar bear push a large, flat rock 100 feet (30 m) across the ground and onto the trigger mechanism of a live trap set for the bear. With the trap sprung, the bear then leisurely ate the bait.

FOODS AND FEEDING BEHAVIOR

Although all bears are technically carnivorous, only the polar bear is almost exclusively a meat eater. Their diet consists mostly of sea mammals such as ringed seals (the most abundant large mammal in the Arctic), bearded seals, and walruses. The bears will also eat shoreline carrion such as beached whales, fish, and crabs. I have read accounts of people seeing up to 100 bears feeding on a dead whale.

Using its superb sense of smell, a polar bear can track its prey across miles of ice.

While out on the ice a polar bear may go without eating for weeks, living off its fat reserves, before it kills a seal. The bear's huge stomach allows it to take full advantage of any temporary windfall. It can load up to 150 pounds (70 kg) of food in a single sitting. To maintain its body weight, however, a polar bear must kill a seal on the average of every five or six days.

If the summertime thaw drives them ashore, the bears may roam the coast looking for food. They will eat baby birds, rodents, reindeer, eggs—practically anything edible—including berries and other plants. Since civilization has arrived in the Arctic, the bears have expanded their taste to include such delicacies as bacon, cheese, engine oil, rubber boots, and the seats of snow machines.

Summer may bring a large variety of food onto a polar bear's menu, but essentially it's a time of weight loss. Tidbits such as fish or Arctic hares may be tasty but they offer little in energy for an animal as big as a polar bear. Throughout the summer and early autumn the bears subsist mainly on stored fat and they slowly lose weight. The difference is made up during the winter seal hunt.

A common hunting technique is to wait patiently by a seal's breathing hole in the ice. Bears have been seen waiting motionless by a hole for up to fourteen hours. When the seal sticks its nose through the hole for a breath of air, the waiting bear springs forward and grabs the animal's head in its jaws, killing it. With incredible strength, the bear stands up with the seal's head firmly clamped in its jaws, jerking the seal through its hole. An adult seal may range from 40 to 60 inches (101 to 152 cm) in length and weigh from 80 to 250 pounds (36 to 113 kg). Sometimes the breathing hole may only be 8 or 10 inches (20 to 25 cm) in diameter, while the seal may be 2 feet (60 cm) or more in diameter. Pulled through this seemingly impossibly small hole, the seal is instantly stretched out into one long spluttering shred of broken bones, blood, and entrails.

Any remains left behind by the bear are quickly scavenged by Arctic foxes, gulls, ravens, or other polar bears. During the winter, the bears may have a retinue of foxes and ravens following them hundreds of miles out on the sea ice, where the scavengers are completely dependent on leftovers for their survival. Occasionally a bear will kill a fox who ventures too close.

Another hunting technique involves quietly stalking a resting seal. When out on the ice, a seal becomes extremely vigilant, staying close to the water and waking from its nap every twenty to thirty seconds to look around. Lowering its head, the seal goes back to sleep for a few more moments before again raising itself to look around. Each time the seal drops its head, the polar bear inches slowly forward, instantly "freezing" when the seal raises its head. The stalk eventually ends in a wild charge when the bear suddenly springs up and bounds forward over the last few yards in an effort to grab and disable the seal before it can slip into the water. For some unexplained reason, some observers claim, the bear always uses its left paw to kill the seal.

Sometimes a polar bear will stalk a resting seal by swimming very slowly toward it. When close enough, the bear will submerge, swim to the edge of the ice floe where the seal is resting, and then explode from the water, cutting off the seal's escape route.

During the spring about half the seals killed are newborn pups. Late in the winter, the seals' breathing holes become covered with snow. If the snow becomes deep enough, the seals will carve out an "igloo" on the ice directly above the breathing hole, where they will rest and give birth to their pups. A polar bear is able to sense exactly where in the seal's chamber the breathing hole is located. When a bear explodes through the den's snow roof, it is nearly always at that spot. If the bear can block the seal's escape route quickly enough, he will have earned a meal. Overall, fewer than 15 percent of a polar bear's hunts will

be successful. Individual hunting success, depending on ice conditions and time of year, varies greatly from bear to bear.

Laying low for the duration of an Arctic storm, a polar bear uses the scant protection afforded by the lee side of a snowbank.

DENNING BEHAVIOR

Although polar bears may construct temporary winter shelters in order to escape severe weather, usually only pregnant females den for any extended period. Males and other bears that do not den may enter a physiological state called "walking hibernation," in which they remain awake and active.

During normal hibernation, bears obtain whatever energy and water they need from metabolizing stored fat. (The daily energy budget of a 440-pound (200-kg) polar bear is equal to the energy value of about two pounds (0.9 kg) of seal blubber (4187 Kcal).) In winter, polar bears also live off fat, but it's seal fat rather than their own body reserves. "If a polar bear were to eat a lot of protein when it's 50° or 60° F (−45° to −51° C) below," says Dr. Jonkel, "then they would need a lot of water in order to get rid of the nitrogen wastes. That would mean they would have to melt the cold snow in their mouths. By restricting food consumption to mostly fat, they circumvent that need." (A few scientists also believe that polar bears may switch to a kind of "conservation metabolism" during the lean months of summer.)

Denning usually begins about mid-October or in early November. Typically, these maternity dens are dug into snowbanks, often on south-facing slopes near the coast. The largest dens may be 3 feet (1 m) high, and over 8 feet wide and 10 feet long (2.5 by 3 m) inside. These chambers are usually oval rooms with an entrance tunnel leading to them. Because of the insulating qualities of snow, the heat given off by a denning bear may raise the den's air temperature to as high as 40° F (4.4° C), even when outside temperatures are far below freezing.

Polar bear denning sites are concentrated in at least seventeen locations over the circumpolar range of the species. One of the world's largest denning areas was discovered in 1969 by Dr. Charles Jonkel in a forest and lake region about 40 miles (64 km) south of Churchill, Manitoba. Also, the Canadian province of Ontario, in an effort to protect its Cape Henrietta Maria denning site, has designated an area of more than 6,000 square miles (15,540 sq km) as a provincial polar bear park.

While bears are in their dens, changes in wind direction may cause the roofs to become thin or even to open, making the dens unsuitable. When that happens the females will leave and either dig temporary dens or reoccupy deserted ones. The proportion of temporary dens is higher in years with little snow. Steve Amstrup, an Alaskan polar-bear researcher, recently discovered that polar bears in the Beaufort Sea area no longer come ashore to den. They now den on the multiyear ice lying far offshore. It is believed that snowmobile activity and hunting along the coast have driven the bears from the land.

Another unique feature of bear ecology in the Churchill area is the use of summer dens. Dug down through the tundra to permafrost, these dens are used as cool retreats for overheated bears. The bears doze away the summer months, lying on the ice, expending a minimum of energy. Some of these dens appear to have been in use for hundreds of years.

REPRODUCTIVE BEHAVIOR

Female polar bears usually breed for the first time at five or six years of age. Mating takes place out on the pack ice during a rather long breeding season extending from late March to about mid-July. An eager throng of fiercely competitive male suitors often follow a female during her time of estrus, which lasts for about three weeks.

After fertilization, the tiny embryo divides a few times and then free floats in the uterus, not to resume development until September, when it finally implants in the uterine wall.

Just prior to denning, pregnant females become particularly fat. They enter their overwintering maternity dens in October or November and give birth to their one to four cubs (twins are most common) sometime during December or January. The igloo-like den is an important barrier against cold. Blind and helpless, the cubs at birth are not much bigger than guinea pigs, weighing only about 20 ounces (.6 kg) each. The sex ratio of newborn cubs appears to be about equal. They remain in the den until late March or April, growing quickly on their mother's milk, which is very rich in fat. Female polar bears have four functional mammary glands.

By the time increasing daylight encourages the family to surface from the den, the cubs may weigh between 22 and 33 pounds (10 to 15 kg). In only two months or so, the cubs have gained twenty-five times their birth weight.

Initially, for up to two weeks, the cubs stay at the den entrance, playing and acclimating to the outside. At the slightest sign of danger the entire family withdraws to the den. When they finally do leave, the cubs are large enough to travel with their mother across the frozen tundra and out onto the sea ice. Having lived only on her fat reserves, the mother is now extremely thin and hungry for seals. After a kill, she consumes the energy-rich blubber and skin first.

The cubs continue to nurse, suckling for about fifteen minutes six or seven times a day, until they are nearly two years old. Before taking a nursing position the mother usually digs a shallow pit in which she lies down. She often nurses while lying on her back, with the cubs on her abdomen. Sometimes she will sit upright and lean forward while her cubs nurse.

Polar bear cubs begin receiving hunting lessons during their first summer. By July, they will have acquired a taste for seal blood and fat. They follow their mother everywhere, riding piggyback on her when she goes swimming.

By August, the cubs weigh over 100 pounds (45 kg). But they are still dependent on their mother and they den with her for one or two more winters. When the family finally does break up, the cubs are usually between twenty-four and twenty-eight months old. However, some families may den together for a fourth winter.

Abandoned by the mother, the half-grown cubs wander about, completely on their own. They may stay together for a short time, but eventually each goes

Bears, even adult polar bears, sometimes exhibit behavior that can only be interpreted as play.

its own way. A high mortality rate faces these young, inexperienced bears during their first year or two alone, but because Hudson Bay is so rich in food, cubs weaned there at the age of two have a good chance of survival. Surviving females reach adult weight by their fifth year and males between years eight and ten.

The usual time span between litters is every three or four years, but in the ideal conditions found there, about 40 percent of the bears on Hudson Bay's west coast breed every second year. Recent studies indicate that some mothers living under the difficult conditions found in other arctic areas may only produce one or two litters in their lifetime.

THE WANDERING BEAR'S ARCTIC REALM

Polar bears roam the frozen seas of all the arctic nations: Russia, Norway, Greenland (Territory of Denmark), Canada, and the United States. Until recently, scientists believed polar bears traveled randomly around the northern part of the globe, so that an individual bear seen near Russia would eventually appear in the Canadian North, later in Alaska, and so on around the globe.

Although they are circumpolar in distribution, most polar bears are now known to belong to geographically discrete populations that remain in the same general area year after year. The bears do travel far, however; in the course of a year's time, some may range over frozen seascapes exceeding 20,000 square miles (51,800 sq km) in area. One marked polar bear was killed a year later some 2,000 miles (3,218 km) away from its original release point.

The Earth's North Polar ice cap and the central core of the Arctic Ocean encircling the North Pole are permanently frozen. But around the fringes of the polar basin, where sea meets land, the ice breaks up each year. This is the polar bear's habitat. Although footprints of wandering polar bears have been seen within two degrees of the North Pole, this is not their usual range, since few seals, or any other animals, live this far north.

Polar bears' and seals' distribution is influenced by the patterns of ice freeze up and breakup. There are approximately six distinct population centers along the southern rim of the polar basin, each with its unique pattern of ice movement: Western Alaska and Wrangel Island, northern Alaska, the Canadian arctic archipelago, Greenland, Svalbard–Franz Josef Land, and central Siberia. A separate subpopulation, far south of the main body of bears, lives in Canada's Hudson and James bays. This is the most southerly group of polar bears in the world.

In the high arctic, bears generally follow the expanding edge of the arctic sea ice as it spreads south in winter. In summer, when the ice retreats to the north, the bears move with it. However, this pattern is not at all clearly defined and there are many exceptions. For example, many bears of the Canadian Arctic spend the summer along the coastline instead of retreating north with the shrinking ice cap. Along Hudson Bay, bears go inland and endure the warmer weather by lying in pits or caves dug down to permafrost.

Although landed polar bears generally stay close to the shore, they have been sighted up to 100 miles (160 km) inland. The distribution of individual bears along the coast seems to be regulated by the dominance hierarchy. Adult males are often found in choice areas close to the beach. Females with cubs stay farther inland and young males and single females farther from the ocean still.

By staying close to its mother, this cub will soon learn the ways of survival in the Arctic. The little bear began to receive hunting lessons during its first summer.

By standing upright, a bear greatly increases its sight distance. A commotion nearly a mile away attracts this one's attention.

Although landed polar bears generally stay close to the shore, they have been sighted up to one hundred miles (160 km) inland.

THE DECLINE AND RESCUE OF THE ICE BEAR

The Eskimo peoples have always killed polar bears. Killing them was considered an act worthy of honor, and the hide and meat were welcome provisions. For several millennia there was no question of overhunting; the bear was too powerful and dangerous, the hunter's weapons too primitive. Then came the European explorers, pushing west and north. As fur traders and whalers began to penetrate the Arctic in the early seventeenth century, the bears were killed in ever-increasing numbers. In Victorian times, parlor rugs made from polar bear skins became a status symbol. Adventurous "sportsmen" and hide hunters carrying modern firearms killed thousands of bears to meet the demand. By 1930, the polar bear was in serious decline. Another thirty years of nearly uncontrolled hunting continued, nearly exterminating the great white bear in northern Russia, Scandinavia, and along the Labrador coast. Polar bears in Alaska were beginning to suffer the same fate.

Finally, in 1967, concern for the bears caused scientists from the five "polar bear" nations to ratify a conservation treaty. Norway and Russia opted to end hunting entirely. The United States and Greenland (Territory of Denmark) limited the killing of polar bears to subsistence hunters. Because Canadian polar bear populations did not seem to be in danger, hunting was still allowed in a quota system, under which some 600 to 700 bears could be killed annually by the Eskimo (Inuit) people, who traditionally hunted them.

Today the bears seem to be experiencing a modest comeback. Their total numbers are estimated to be somewhere between 20,000 and 40,000 animals worldwide. Canada has approximately 15,000 polar bears, possibly two-thirds of the world's total. Most of them live in the northern Northwest Territories.

Polar bears may have been saved from extinction, but there are remaining problems affecting their survival. In Canada, non-Native sport hunters are allowed to "buy" into the Eskimos' quotas, paying upward of $15,000 (Canadian) for the privilege of a twelve-day hunt. The fee is distributed among the guides, helpers, and the community council, and these hunts and the sale of hides taken on Native quotas have become an important source of revenue for many settlements. But in some areas, the quotas may have been set too high. Canadian bear-biologist Mitch Taylor voices his concern:

> People are aware of the problem now. The Inuit who hunt bears are cooperative and in agreement with our management programs. If we suggest a quota reduction, they would like to see it done in a way that doesn't penalize them . . . but I think we are heading for real management problems. . . . We may have populations that are nearing the depletion level in places where we have been overharvesting for ten or fifteen years. Polar bears have an extremely low capability of sustaining a harvest. Only 1.5 percent of the total population of adult females can be harvested each year . . . if you take more than that, the population declines. The problem is that the decline is so gradual that it's virtually undetectable until the bears have been reduced to the point that you have a numerical effect on the number taken, and then there's a quick drop off.

Canada's quotas were originally established in part by reviewing the fur records of the Hudson's Bay Company to see where and how many polar bears were taken each year. But during those times people weren't concentrated in settlements as much as they are now. "One of the things we'll probably have to do," Mitch Taylor explains, "is to review all of the quotas and try to bring them more into line with what we think the population can sustain." Already some northern communities are asking for compensation for reductions in polar bear quotas.

Alaska's polar bears may be in much more serious trouble. Alaskan Natives have exclusive rights to hunt polar bears without a bag limit and without a closed season. No one knows how many bears are killed because reporting is completely voluntary. A letter sent to me by a friend describes an incident in Kaktovik on Barter Island:

> A bowhead whale was killed by the Eskimos and dragged to shore and cut up. Seven polar bears showed up for the meat hanging in this village of 300 and were killed. Later, another four met the same fate. They can indiscriminately kill as many animals as they want. This is the major reason why the Alaska Fish and Game Department has applied to regain management of the state's marine mammals. (Polar bears are considered marine mammals.)

A warning sign on the outskirts of Churchill, Manitoba.

The Polar Bears of Churchill

One area where polar bears are doing very well is along the western shore of Hudson Bay. This is also one of the best places to see these big bears. Hudson Bay is a huge body of water, about 800 miles wide and 1,000 miles long (1,287 km by 1,609 km), or about twice the size of Texas. During the winter, when it freezes over, the bears live some 40 to 150 miles (64 to 241 km) out on the ice, hunting seals along the leads. When the spring comes, large pieces of ice, called floes, are blown south to ground themselves on the bay's southern shore. The bears ride the floating ice onto the beach and by July have dispersed inland along the coast. As summer advances, they begin the long walk northward, back along the coast to where the seals are. This trek may be 800 to 900 miles long (1,287 to 1,448 km). The bears continue along the western shore until they return to Hudson Bay's northwestern coast, where, in late autumn, they wait for the ice to refreeze. By mid-October some 600 to 1,000 bears are massed along a 100-mile (160-km)-long stretch of coast between the Nelson and Churchill rivers, forming the largest concentration of polar bears in the world. Many of the bears, mostly males, cluster on headlands and capes, especially Cape Churchill. When the first hard freezes occur in November, the bears disperse out over the frozen bay in search of seals.

The town of Churchill, Canada's northernmost deepwater port, lies right in the path of the migrating polar bears, and every autumn polar bears can be seen meandering around this community of about 800 people. For the last ten years or so a polar bear alert system has been set up in town to discourage marauding bears and to ensure people's safety. Everyone is taught from childhood on how to avoid or deal with bears. Bears that approach within a certain distance of the town or are caught rummaging through the municipal dump are captured and put into a holding facility, where great care is taken to make sure the bears do not get used to being around people while they are in "jail." The bears are watered but not fed, since they can go months without eating. As soon as the bay freezes, the twenty or thirty bears that are detained each year are tranquilized and transported away from town by helicopter. This is an excellent, but expensive, alternative to shooting nuisance bears.

Actually, Churchill residents are quite proud of their bears, calling their village the "Polar Bear Capitol of the World." Hundreds of tourists now travel to Churchill every year just to see the bears, and the town's guest facilities are full from late September to mid-November. For about a month, polar bear tours are big business in Churchill. Monstrous-sized tundra buggies with huge tires, said to be gentle on the surrounding tundra, take loads of thrilled tourists and

Immobilized by drugs, a polar bear in a net sling is being airlifted away from the town of Churchill for release out on the ice of Hudson Bay.

Spray-painted letters help conservation officers and researchers to keep tabs on a bear that habitually approaches human dwellings. The markings will disappear when the bear's winter coat is shed.

Safely enclosed in a steel cage, a re-search assistant at Cape Churchill ob-serves the movements of a polar bear mother and her cub.

An armed tundra-buggy guard keeps a wary eye on a curious polar bear.

wildlife photographers out among the waiting bears. Tourist season abruptly ends when the bay finally freezes over and the bears suddenly vanish.

About 40 or 50 miles (64 to 80 km) south of Churchill stands the Cape Churchill Research Tower. When I flew out to visit this remote spot, the tower was being used for a bear-deterrent program headed by Peter Clarkson of the Northwest Territories Department of Renewable Resources, who was testing ways of deterring polar bears without harming them. (A discussion on bear deterrents can be found in chapter 9.) My journal records the view from the top of the 100-foot (30-m)-high structure:

> The land is desolate, gray, flat . . . the eye reaches out toward the horizon, which is filtered and fuzzy; not really a line at all . . . this must be the most desolate spot I have ever been in. The only human activity is here, at the tower, and it rarely goes beyond a few feet from its base. We are alone, standing here . . . the only movement is the wind, our constant compan-ion. My eyes water from the strain of looking for something to see in this forbidding land. And then it comes . . . the sudden ghost-like appearance of the white bear, moving silently, steadily, across the gravel and ice-cov-ered landscape.

Hudson Bay froze over while I was out at the tower. It was an experience I shall never forget. Day after day, for over a week, the temperature kept drop-ping and the wind became stronger. As the temperature plummeted and the wind howled, the surface of the bay became slushy. But the wind and waves prevented the particles of slush from freezing together. The temperature, with the chill factor, dropped to −120° C (−184° F). I became ill with bronchial problems and we lost most of our heat. The weather was too rough for the chopper to come in and drop supplies, so we just had to wait and sit out the storm. Once, while I was climbing back up the tower from our ground-based outhouse, I froze my nose. As the cold sapped our warmth, we began to take turns at hunkering over an oil heater that sometimes worked, sometimes didn't. The jokes finally stopped and our faces turned grim. The two-way radio had broken. I was wishing that I had remained back in town with the tourists. Darkness was nearly on us, when we finally heard over the noise of the shaking tower the ''thump, thump, thump'' of a helicopter. Our pilot, Steve Miller, had chanced it and had found a hole in the storm through which he could fly out to us with fuel and supplies and to take me back to civilization.

The wind stopped sometime during the night, and the next day dawned absolutely clear and sunny. The storm had been one of the coldest blows in Churchill's history. As soon as the wind had stopped, Hudson Bay's superchilled surface froze solid. Although I was still very ill and coughing, I was so amazed at the transformation that I managed to walk over a mile out onto the ice. Flying along the coast with his helicopter, Steve Miller reported later that he could see the polar bears dispersing out onto the bay. By 1:00 P.M. there was not a polar bear to be seen anywhere on land.

Safe on the deck of a tundra-buggy, a group of tourists thrill to see a wild polar bear. Each year hundreds of people travel to Churchill to see the bears' annual migration.

POLAR BEAR PALS AND PLAYMATES

The image we have of solitary polar bears wandering alone across the frozen expanses of the North is not necessarily accurate. Sometimes two bears, usually males, will form "friendships" that last for weeks, perhaps years.

"Sometimes it's two or three big guys," says bear-researcher Mitch Taylor.

> Occasionally they'll have a kid along, a subadult. No one really knows how long they may stick together, but these are definite social units. If you chase them in a helicopter, they stick together like a mother with cubs. Sometimes when we drug one bear in order to put a radio transmitter on it, the other bear will come up and lick its feet and then lay down against it.

The friendly bears may feed and travel together or even form "play" groups. As a rule only fat bears play. Fred Bruemmer, in his 1984 article "How Polar

Bears Break the Ice'' in *Natural History,* eloquently describes the bears' play behavior:

A bear that wishes to play slowly approaches another suitable male, and the two begin a massive, slow-motion minuet. They circle and sniff, heads low, mouths closed, eyes averted, and they are silent, signaling by attitude and posture peaceful intent and mutual respect. . . . They ''mouth'' each other with jaws wide open or chew gently at each other's necks like horses grooming each other. One places a . . . paw upon the other's shoulder, they rise and spar and push, lose balance and embrace, sway and wrestle. One topples and lies on his back, huge paws pedaling in the air. The other, jaws agape, throws himself on top and they romp on the ground, then rise and wrestle again. Considering their awesome power, the bears practice marvelous restraint and are extremely careful not to hurt each other. Each bout lasts about 15 minutes. . . . Toward the end both bears are panting so loudly that they can be heard a hundred yards away [100 m]. Hot and exhausted, they move apart, stretch out on snow or ice like a rug-to-be, gulp snow to cool their overheated bodies, and rest awhile.

A pair of polar bear playmates wrestle on the snow. Not much is known about these friendships, how they form or how long they last.

FUTURE RESEARCH

The data resulting from polar bear research is shared with all polar-bear-management treaty countries. Some of the research projects presently under way include radio-telemetry studies using transmitters that are monitored via satellite to provide information on movement patterns. Tetracycline is being tested as a marker to accurately determine previous captures. (When the drug is injected in small doses, it leaves a tiny deposit in the bones.) Conservation work in Norway has allowed that country's polar bear population to rise almost to its original numbers. And deterrents are being developed that are designed to repel polar bears from humans without hurting the animals.

International research and management programs are key factors in maintaining viable populations of polar bears on this planet.

''TROPICAL'' BEARS

Sun, Sloth, and Spectacled Bears

Bears are usually thought of as creatures of the Northern Hemisphere, but three species range quite close to the equator. In fact, two species, the spectacled bear and the sun bear, actually occur south of the equator. Very little is known about the lives and habits of tropical bears, perhaps because wildlife research is not a high priority for the relatively poor countries in which these bears occur. No one doubts the importance of conservation and wildlife study, but the governments of many Third World nations often simply have no money for long-range resource planning let alone for wildlife research. For this reason, the International Union for the Conservation of Nature (IUCN) and its associate, the World Wildlife Fund, have been major financiers for conservation in the Third World, underwriting recovery programs for such critically endangered species as orangutans, pandas, tigers, elephants, and rhinos.

SUN BEARS: THE WORLD'S SMALLEST BEARS

In the rush to save other animal superstars, this little 100-pound (45-kg) bear has been sadly overlooked. It seldom rates even a footnote in most wildlife studies, and all the information published on it would hardly fill two typewritten pages. Yet what little data there is is disturbing: In 1978 the IUCN included the Sun Bear *(Helarctos malayanus)* on its red-list of endangered species.

Although its populations have been greatly decreased by hunting, the sun bear still exists in the forests of the Malay Peninsula, Java, Sumatra, Burma, and

Young sun bears seem to delight in tree climbing.

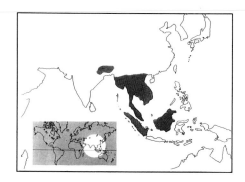

Thailand. In Borneo, the bears have been reported up to 4,900 feet (1,500 m) in the Sabah/Sarawak border region and at 7,500 feet (2,300 m) on Mount Kinabalu.

In 1983, Dr. John Paine of the World Wildlife Fund conducted a survey of the mammals in Sabah. "Sun bears were common nowhere," he reports. "Individuals were seen only twice during the faunal survey and fresh signs only three times . . . however, old claw marks were found in six of the survey areas." Dr. Paine feels it takes a large, continuous block of forest of more than 24,700 acres (10,000 ha) to sustain a sun bear.

To find out more about the sun bears' status, I began sending questionnaires and letters to zoos and scientists around the globe. After more than a year of correspondence, I still had few leads. "In 1960 several sun bears in Thailand were captured and sold to zoos," one informant wrote. "This was the last record I could find of sun bears being obtained from the wild." A week later I received a letter from the World Wildlife Fund Data Center in Bangalore, India, informing me that the sun bear was now considered extinct on that subcontinent. My hopes of ever seeing and photographing sun bears in the wild were quickly evaporating.

Then one evening a surprise telephone call put me in touch with a team of zoologists recently returned from Borneo. One of the men on the team had been bitten on the leg by a sun bear as he had stood reading a trail map. After biting the man, the bear had vanished into the jungle as suddenly as it had appeared.

In some parts of Southeast Asia sun bears have a reputation of being as dangerous as an enraged elephant. So I wasn't at all sure what kind of animal we would be dealing with, if and when we finally found one of these creatures in the wild. But Borneo seemed to be our best bet for locating the sun bear's last stronghold, so photographer Mark Newman and I decided to go there and find it.

Acting on the advice of Dr. Alan Rabinowitz of the New York Zoological Society, we made our way to Sabah, Borneo's most northern territory. Dr. Rabinowitz had heard hunters' stories about sun bears in this region and had even seen captive pets there. What we found when we arrived was at once hopeful and disheartening.

The Situation in Sabah

The government of Malaysia (of which Sabah is a state) has been progressive enough to have set aside several national parks and forest reserves. The World Wildlife Fund has also done some significant work in the country in an effort to save orangutans from extinction. Because the sun bear is an endangered species, hunting them is no longer allowed in Malaysia, or anywhere else for that matter.

However, in Borneo and in the rest of Southeast Asia, conservation laws are not always enforceable. Poaching has long been and still is a time-honored occupation over much of this region. Most of the bears that come into captivity are by this illegal method; the mothers are shot and the cubs brought back as pets. Borneo's few wildlife wardens try to prosecute poachers, but they can do very little to stop the practice since only about twenty rangers cover the entire state of Sabah. (About 28,500 square miles in size, Sabah is nearly the size of South Carolina.)

As we moved through the country, going from town to town, we tried to meet as many local people as we could. Because we bought a lot of beer as we attempted to gain bits of information about sun bears, we called our campaign our "barroom research." It wasn't until our reputation began to precede us that people started to trust us and provide us with useful information.

The Poaching Problem

Assured that we weren't going to turn them over to the game wardens, some people eventually introduced us to a poacher who was willing to tell us about his hunting methods. His stories, told in a matter-of-fact way, seemed to indicate that he saw nothing wrong with his activities. As he spoke, a larger pattern began to reveal itself.

One of Borneo's greatest natural resources is its forests of giant tropical hardwoods. To harvest this wealth, the trees must be cut down and made into lumber. Once a region is opened up for logging and the logs have been hauled away, the remaining road system provides easy access for poachers. A common hunting method is to drive a pickup truck along these back roads at night while sweeping the surrounding area with a spotlight. (Back in the United States this illegal hunting technique is called "jacklighting.") When the light shines on an animal, its eyes reflect a bright glow to the shooters sitting in the back of the truck. The light also dazzles the animal momentarily—just long enough for it to be blasted with a shotgun.

We were shown evidence of the kill from one recent hunt. Thrown together in a great bloody heap were some of the rarest and most beautiful jungle animals in the world. A bearded pig lay at the bottom of the pile, then came two sambour deer, two clouded leopards, a sun bear, and two species of civit cats. Mark and I were nearly speechless as the hunter showed us photo after photo of past kills. Patrick Andau, Sabah's chief game warden, says many of these illegal kills are sold to profitable meat syndicates.

Sony, Our Borneo Bear

During our stay in Borneo we found nine sun bears, six of them under two years old. Unfortunately, all the bears we saw were in captivity, some of them

A subadult sun bear pauses momentarily from its digging efforts at the base of a jungle tree.

Young sun bears make energetic and engaging pets. In order to obtain cubs, however, hunters usually kill the mothers.

A captive sun bear is totally engrossed in extracting the contents from a jar of honey. This species' fondness for the sweet liquid has prompted locals to call them "honey bears."

as illegal pets. Whenever it can, the Malaysian government confiscates wild birds and animals being kept this way, then releases them in remote areas with the hope that the bears' familiarity with humans will not make them easy targets for poachers.

One day we followed one of the recently released sun bears into the jungle to photograph it and to observe its behavior in its natural habitat. For the better part of a week we followed that bear, most of the time on our hands and knees while looking out for leeches and pythons. The young bear, whom we nicknamed "Sony," quickly became used to our presence. Each morning we would lead him farther and farther down a jungle trail away from the outpost. Sony soon ignored us and began to forage for food.

Sun bears are extremely difficult to study in the wild. They are scarce and very cautious. Usually it is dusk when they set out on methodical explorations of their hunting range for anything edible: fruit, honey, snails, eggs, lizards, rodents, termites. Feeding signs such as prominent claw marks on the trunk of a tree or a shredded rotten log are often the only evidence of their activities.

Luckily, we were able to watch Sony for hours as he moved across the jungle floor searching for food. The most remarkable aspect of his search was its incredible speed. Unlike northern ecosystems, tropical forests offer very little in the way of large, concentrated supplies of food, or "ecocenters." (A run of salmon is a good example of an ecocenter.) Food in the jungle is thinly spread through the forest. And since fallen fruit and dead animals rot quickly in the warm, humid environment, there are few opportunities for stumbling across a rich feast.

In order to maximize his effort, Sony would skim across the jungle floor, stopping only long enough to eat some tidbit or tear at a fallen log. Northern bears also attempt to maximize their foraging efforts, but not at the speed of this sun bear. His energetic skimming behavior may be a clue as to how these omnivorous animals are able to find enough food to survive.

Vital Statistics

Apparently, the sun bear *(Helarctos malayanus)* gets its name from the yellowish crescent on its chest. This mark varies in size from bear to bear and sometimes may not be present at all. In some areas of their range, sun bears are known as honey bears or Malay bears. Weighing between 60 and 143 pounds (27 to 65 kg) this smallest member of the bear tribe grows to only about 4.5 feet (137 cm) in length. In the wild, a sun bear weighing over 110 pounds (50 kg) is considered big.

The sun bear is covered with short, dense, black fur that at first glance seems too thick for an animal living in the warm tropics. But as we watched Sony forage, I was surprised at how efficiently the bear's fur shed rain, mud, and other debris. At the end of each day, when Mark and I emerged from the jungle, we would be smeared with dirt and sweat from head to toe. Our sun bear would come out spotless.

This sleek and compact animal's muzzle may vary from grayish white to orange in color. It has small, rather beady, eyes and small, rounded ears. The feet, tipped with long sickle-shaped claws, are sometimes colored with gray and have no hair on their soles. Its short bowlegs give it an ungainly appearance when walking. Like other bears, the sun bear often stands up on its hind legs to get a better view of a distant object or when it encounters a potential enemy.

Notes on Sun Bear Behavior

The sun bear is said to be one of the most dangerous animals a human can encounter in the jungle. Besides biting with its powerful jaws, it sometimes tears at its opponent with its sharp claws. I have been told by natives that even a tiger will leave a sun bear alone. If a larger predator grabs a sun bear, the bear

Growing not much larger than this village dog, sun bears are the world's smallest species of bear.

Wild sun bears often leave scratch marks in trees as a sign of their activity and possibly to declare their presence in the area.

is able to turn around in its loose skin to bite back. Sun bears also have the reputation of being one of the few animals that will charge without apparent cause. It barks loudly when on the attack. As with most bears, however, the sun bear's ferocious reputation is probably exaggerated. Young sun bears are extremely playful and make very appealing pets until they become too large. (Sony was the most energetic and delightful animal I have ever been around.)

An expert climber, the usually nocturnal sun bear spends much of its day sleeping or sunbathing in trees between 6.5 feet and 23 feet (2 to 7 m) above the ground. It is said to make its bed in a small platform made of broken branches. The nest looks similar to the nests of orangutans but are usually nearer to the tree trunk and more loosely made. Often traveling in pairs, sun bears are occasionally seen foraging on the ground during the day.

Sun bears have a varied diet that includes eating any small rodent, lizard, small bird, or insect it can find. Bees, termites, and earthworms form a large part of their diet. Sun bears also eat the heart of coconut palms, the large growing "bud" at the top of the tree. Since removal of the heart usually kills the tree, a bear may inflict serious damage to a coconut plantation by feeding on palm hearts. Sometimes a marauding bear will return to the plantation night after night until all the trees have been affected. Sun bears are also extremely fond of honey and will tear open trees to find bees' nests, which they eat comb, grubs, and all.

Sun bears, especially cubs, often suck their paws while making a "humming" sound. This behavior has been described as a sign of contentment but is more likely a kind of displacement activity, like thumb-sucking with human children. Adult bears sometimes utter hoarse grunts and loud roars that may be confused with those of the adult male orangutan. No evidence of hibernation behavior has ever been observed with sun bears.

Reproduction

Females first breed in their third year. Courtship generally lasts from two days to a week, anytime during the year, and includes such behavior as barking, hugging, mock fighting, head bobbing, and kissing. The average pregnancy is about 100 days. In the wild, sunbears are thought to give birth to their

Moving at a rapid pace, a sun bear quickly digs into decayed wood during its seemingly endless search for food.

In a rare natural jungle clearing, a sun bear consumes some small invertebrates it has discovered.

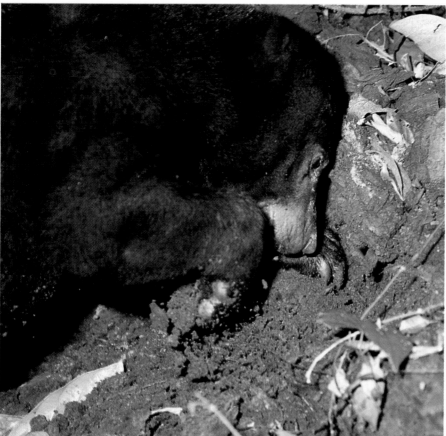

Foraging across the forest floor, sun bears eat practically anything edible they find.

In the leafy gloom, far below Borneo's jungle forest canopy, a sun bear tears at a rotting log.

twin cubs on the ground, well hidden in the vegetation of the forest floor.

The newborn cubs are tiny, weighing only some 7 ounces (225 grams), and are blind and hairless. At birth their skin is nearly transparent. During their first two weeks the cubs are unable to walk, but in a few months they will have become strong enough to run and play, and may be weaned at that time. The cubs usually accompany their mother until nearly grown. Some reports suggest that sun bears may form monogamous pairs in the wild. Pairs of adults have been seen accompanied by infants.

The Future for Borneo's Bears

Extensive logging is chopping Borneo's forests into ever-smaller chunks. It may also be changing the climate of the region. Borneo has been experiencing long-term droughts so severe that in some places the rain forest has become dry enough to burn. In Kalimantan, central Borneo, a devastating forest fire burned uncontrolled for nearly a year. Even in Sabah, brush fires have been common during the past few years.

As Mark and I headed for Sabah's international airport, with the knowledge that at least sun bears still existed, I noticed some headlines on an English edition Malaysian newpaper. The large black type proudly crowed, "TIMBER BOOM IS BACK! Sabah log prices up 50%. Exports Soaring." Bad news for the forest and its bears.

An Encouraging Note

At home, in the heap of mail that had accumulated in my long absence, lay a ragged, badly typed envelope. Its return address was "Zoological Survey of India," and in it was a letter from S. M. Ali, a wildlife and conservation scientist, that stated:

> The sun bear is still surviving in the North Eastern region of India, and its population is quite satisfactory in and around Blue Mountain in Chimtuipui district of Mizoram as observed during January and February 1987. Further sighting records . . . confirm its occurrence in Namdhapa Tiger Preserve in Tirup district of Arunachal Pradesh. It is also expected to occur in Manipur, Nagaland and Tripura as well.

Apparently, sun bears have been rediscovered in India.

Sun bears will readily climb trees to reach ripening fruit or succulent leaves.

Sloth Bears: Energetic Denizens of Southeast Asia

Toward the end of the eighteenth century the first pelts of the sloth bear arrived in Europe. Shot by big-game hunters in India, the skins were accompanied by notes asserting that the animals had trunklike snouts and were in the habit of hanging upside down in the branches of jungle trees for hours on end. They were also said to cry like a child.

Dr. George Shaw of the British Museum, influenced by these descriptions and the animal's long sickle-shaped claws, classified the animal among the sloths. However, in 1810, when a live specimen reached Paris, it was realized that this animal wasn't a sloth at all but a bear, and a very active one at that. The name "bear sloth" was quickly reversed to "sloth bear" and it stuck.

The "Unbearlike" Bear

The typical sloth bear *(Melursus ursinus)* has a long, shaggy, unkempt, black coat, with a prominent white or yellow chevron or *Y* marking on its chest. The hair is longer and shaggier than other bears', particularly on the back of the neck and between the shoulders, which gives the sloth bear a maned appearance. The belly and underleg hair is sparse, possibly to help cool the animal on hot days.

Its long, dirty white or gray muzzle is equipped with extremely protrusible lips and with nostrils that can be closed voluntarily. The bear has no front teeth, and the bony palate is hollowed out. These adaptations allow the bear to form an efficient vacuum tube with its lips to suck termites (its staple food) out of their galleries. Also, the reduced hair on the muzzle may be a special adaptation for coping with termites' sticky defense secretions.

The feet have white, blunt, curved claws up to 3 inches (7.6 cm) long. The palms and areas between the pads are somewhat bald, and the pads of the fingertips are united by hairless webs. Sloth bears grow to be about 6 feet (1.8 m) long, and stand 3 feet (91 cm) high at the shoulder. They have a 6- to 7-inch (16- to 18-cm)-long tail. Big males can weigh up to 300 pounds (136 kg). Females are generally smaller.

Range and Distribution

Somewhere between 7,000 and 10,000 sloth bears are estimated to still exist in the world. They are found in the forested areas on the island of Sri Lanka and the Indian subcontinent, northward to the base of the Himalayas, and eastward to Assam. They are also known to occur in Nepal's Chitwan National Park. Within its range, the sloth bear inhabits a wide variety of forest types, ranging from the thorn forests of northern India to the wet tropical forests in the south. Common in India two decades ago, today the sloth bear appears to be rapidly disappearing over most of its range. Widespread land clearing and deforestation seem to be most responsible for the bear's declining numbers.

There is one bright note to this dismal picture, however. India's national effort to protect the Bengal tiger is also helping to conserve sloth bears and other rare animals that also inhabit the reserves. In Corbett Tiger Reserve, the number of sloth bears is actually on the increase.

Sloth bears seem to enjoy sleeping and resting in the full heat of the sun.

General Habits of the Vocal Sloth Bear

Sloth bears are mainly nocturnal, but can be active at any hour during the day. Their usual gait is a slow, shambling walk, but when frightened, they can break into a gallop, moving faster than a running person. Although they are excellent climbers, sloth bears do not climb trees to escape danger.

Although they are not aggressive, a short-range surprise encounter with a sloth bear can be dangerous. Apparently, sloth bears become so intent on whatever they are doing at the time that it is not difficult for a person to stumble upon them, especially at night. The bear's usual response is a spectacular bluff charge terminating in a roaring, upright display. But sometimes the encounter may turn into a tragic mauling before the panicked bear rushes off. Probably the best defense, once contact is made, is to play dead.

Sloth bears seem to like the company of other sloth bears, communicating among themselves with facial expressions and a bizarre range of roars, howls, squeals, yelps, huffs, rattles, and gurgles. They are especially noisy when mating. When resting, they may pass the time buzzing and humming while sucking a paw. They seem very tolerant of heat and often fall asleep in the full light of the tropical sun. The male bears mark trees by scraping the trunks with their forepaws and then rubbing the trunk with their flanks. The habit may be a way of announcing to potential mates that there is an adult male in the area.

This species enters periods of reduced activity but is not known to truly hibernate. In zoos, this period of relative inactivity generally extends from September through January, with December being the peak month. In the wild, sloth bears are said to retreat to caves during long rainy periods.

Left: As a special adaptation for feeding on termites, the sloth bear has no front teeth and its upper palate is hollowed to form an efficient sucking tube when its mouth is closed.

The sloth bear's long muzzle is extremely flexible, and its nostrils can be closed voluntarily to keep out biting ants and termites.

Feeding Habits

The sloth bear's specialized snout makes it an expert termite hunter. (Termite and ant colonies are some of the most abundant and stable food sources found in the tropics.) To get at them the bear digs into the termites' hard mound. When the hard claylike wall finally breaks, the bear inserts its muzzle and blows violently, driving away dust and debris. Then, with an enormous sucking breath, it vacuums up the luckless termites and their larvae. This staccato sucking and blowing can be heard up to 200 yards (182 m) away.

Sloth bears are good climbers and often scale trees to shake down fruit or to raid a bees' nest. Honey is an especially favored food. An article in London's 1977 *Journal of Zoology* describes how sloth bears obtain the sweet stuff:

> On four occasions, all in March, bears were seen in trees feeding on honeycombs which hung from the underside of branches. Using the claws as hooks, the bears can climb large diameter trunks. They descend by sliding backwards, sometime making use of hanging creepers. On one occasion a bear was seen straddling a horizontal branch using a forepaw to scoop up honeycomb from below the branch and periodically wiping the bees from his face.

Although the bears may cry in pain when stung by angry bees, they will persist until all the honeycomb has been eaten. Their other foods include ants, berries, and the occasional scavenged tiger kill. Sloth bears often raid fields of cultivated sugarcane, corn (maize) or cultivated yams. They need abundant water and are said to drink at least once a day, in the evening, during the summer.

Sloth bears have a particular liking for the fleshy flowers of the Mohwa tree (*Madhuca latifolia*). In India, from late March into early May, there is great competition between bears and people for the flowers, as villagers collect large quantities of these cream-colored blossoms for making an alcoholic beverage.

To suck ants and termites from their galleries, sloth bears alternately blow away debris and then suck in mightily to vacuum up the insects.

Equipped with long claws for digging in sun-baked soil, this captive sloth bear's rumpled, shaggy coat is typical of its species.

Reproduction

In Sri Lanka, sloth bears have been observed breeding at all times of the year. In India, the mating season runs from April through June. Sloth bear courtship is a very boisterous affair and includes much hugging and mock fighting.

The gestation period varies from six to seven months. Because most births occur in December or early January, it is possible that these bears experience delayed embryo implantation. Usually two, sometimes three, small cubs are born in a cave or shelter dug under a boulder. They are born blind and remain so for about three weeks. When the cubs are about four or five weeks old, the maternity lair is abandoned.

Sloth bear mothers regularly carry their young to and from the feeding grounds on their backs. The young cubs cling to her shaggy hair and if alarmed bury their faces in her fur. The cubs rarely, if ever, change their riding position. For example, one cub might always ride on the mother's shoulders, the other clinging to her rump. If an accidental reversal should occur, a fight and a mad scramble for positions almost invariably follows. The mother sloth bear may carry her young until they are nearly a third her size.

Adult male sloth bears are unusually gentle toward cubs and have even been seen traveling in family groups; villagers in India believe the father helps to raise his offspring. The only prolonged associations noted by scientists, however, have been between mothers and cubs. The cubs usually stay with their mother for two or three years.

The Future of the Sloth Bear

In India, sloth bears are not considered game animals. For the most part, they are tolerated by villagers and are killed only when they become persistent crop raiders. Thus the main threat to the bear's existence, as with most animals in India, is the human destruction of and interference in their habitat. Timber cutting is especially harmful.

Spectacled Bears: The Short-faced Bear of South America

The only species of bear living in South America, spectacled bears *(Tremarctos ornatus)*, are the sole survivors of a subfamily of short-faced bears that ranged across North and South America during the last Ice Age. Today they are found only in the Andes from Venezuela to Chile.

General Description

Spectacled bears get their name from the light-colored rings around the eyes that sometimes look like eyeglasses. These tawny markings vary greatly from bear to bear and sometimes extend from the cheeks to the chest. Often the pattern is only a half-circle around the eyes. The rest of the coat is black and somewhat shaggy in appearance.

Adults weigh from 175 to 275 pounds (80 to 125 kg) and stand about 30 inches (76 cm) high at the shoulder when on all fours. Average lengths are between 4.25 and 6.25 feet (1.3 to 1.9 m). Males are larger and more robust, attaining weights up to 385 pounds (175 kg) and lengths of over 7.25 feet (2.2 m), not including a short tail about 3 inches (7 cm) long. Spectacled bears have only thirteen pairs of ribs—one less than other bears. It has a comparatively large skull equipped with strong teeth and powerful jaws.

Distribution of the Spectacled Bear

Within its Andean range, small populations of spectacled bears can be found from coastal deserts at 600 feet (180 m) all the way up to 13,800 feet (4,200 m) at the snow line. In Ecuador, on the western slopes of the Andes, a few bears are still present in the protected areas of Cayambe-Coca National Park. Conservation efforts to protect the only known travel corridor for spectacled bears between the central and eastern Andean ranges has begun to receive some support. A recently created interagency committee coordinates government actions in the historical sanctuary at Machu Picchu, Peru. On the eastern side of the Andes, where their habitat is less vulnerable to colonization, the bears are reported to be more numerous.

Spectacled bears have also been found in Venezuela, Colombia, and Bolivia. Some researchers believe it is possible that spectacled bears still survive in some groups in a few isolated areas in Panama, Brazil, and Argentina, but this has not yet been confirmed.

Spectacled Bears and Humans

The ancient Incas happily coexisted with the spectacled bear until the arrival of the Spaniards, who considered the bear a symbol of machismo. In the 1800s, it was a popular sport to run bears down on horseback and spear them. After slaying a spectacled bear, the hunters would drink its blood in the belief it would impart some of the animal's strength.

Today the spectacled bear, also known as the Andean bear and *ucumari,* is a rare and endangered species over most of its range. Although it is difficult to estimate their numbers, perhaps as few as 2,000 of these bears still exist in the wild. To augment the 100 or so spectacled bears living in captivity, a number of zoos have begun coordinated breeding programs.

The rich lowland savannas, benchlands, and foothills where spectacled bears were once abundant have long been claimed for agriculture. The few remaining bears live in isolated, dense forests on steep mountainsides. However, because of a massive exodus of farmers leaving land that can no longer support them, people are starting to move into even these last wilderness strongholds, destroying both the forests and its bears as they clear the land. Because spectacled bears often raid maize fields, pesticides containing parathion are sometimes applied over the tops of the cornstalks in an effort to poison them; whole families of bears are sometimes wiped out this way. Spectacled bears are blamed for eating up to half of the crop in some agricultural areas.

Whenever they are encountered, spectacled bears are killed. Hunters have recently discovered that bear parts can be quite valuable; a bear paw may be worth as much as $10 or $20 (US), and a liter of bear fat, a folk remedy for arthritis, may bring as much as $6. Protection and conservation of the spectacled bear is extremely difficult because of the extensive area to be patrolled and numerous political problems, which usually preclude any legal action against poachers.

Spectacled bears receive their name from these unique facial markings, which often encircle their eyes like glasses.

Human settlements are the chief cause for the isolation and fragmentation of remaining spectacled bear populations. Over time this isolation could cause widespread inbreeding problems affecting the genetic vitality of the species. According to Bernie Peyton, a U.S. researcher who has spent the last several years trying to attract more scientific attention to these bears, the effects of inbreeding are already being seen. In the desert areas of Peru, the bears used to weigh over 440 pounds (200 kg) and have from two to four cubs. Now they weigh an average of only about 85 pounds (39 kg) and almost never have more than one cub.

Foraging Strategies and Other Habits

The spectacled bear is more of a vegetarian than most other bears. In addition to fruit, sugarcane, corn, and honey, these bears include in their diet an array of plants so tough to chew that few other animals can eat them. Unopened palm leaves, palm nuts, cactus, orchid pseudobulbs, and bromeliad hearts are a few items on this list. In Venezuela, at certain places above 9,800 feet (3,000 m), the bears commonly eat the white central part of the trunks and leaf bases of puya *(Puya aristiguietae)*, a large variety of terrestrial bromeliad resembling a giant pineapple top. The plant's tough, spiny leaves are stripped away, as we would eat an artichoke.

Apparently, the best habitat left for spectacled bears lies between the low jungle forests containing fruit trees and the high cloud forests. Most of the bears' year is spent in this zone, though they occasionally emerge above tree line to feed on berries, bromeliads, and plants in the groundsel *(Espeletia)* family.

Like all bears, spectacled bears take advantage of any concentrated food source and will eat other animals if given an opportunity. This may include rabbits, ants, mice, birds, llamas, and domestic cattle. At certain times of the year, meat can make up as much as 7 percent of their diet. (Spectacled bears will be even more carnivorous if given a chance. Some fall into the habit of killing a domestic cow every two or three days and will continue to do so until they are killed by outraged farmers.)

Although numerous tales have been told about their ferocity, in reality spectacled bears are quite timid. When traveling, they typically use ridge lines and steep ravines, avoiding the lower valleys because of possible human contact. After seven years of slashing through the forest in search of these elusive bears,

Said to be the most arboreal of all bears, spectacled bears are excellent climbers and seem to be just as much at home in the tree tops as on the ground.

Like all bears, spectacled bears will stand on two legs in order to get a better view of something. Here you can see the species' short facial profile.

Bernie Peyton says that he has seen only eight. Their relatively short legs enable them to slip with ease through dense vegetation that is impassible to humans.

Spectacled bears are excellent tree climbers and spend considerable amounts of time sleeping and eating in fruit trees. Because some trees produce nearly all their fruit in only three or four days, the bears may remain aloft through a tree's whole fruit-ripening period in order to take advantage of this temporary abundance. Often a convenient "daybed" is set up at the junction of the trunk and the first major branch. If a tree has fruit on branches that will not support the bear's weight, the animal will creep out as far as it feels comfortable and then bend the branches back toward itself in order to reach the fruit; ten or twenty branches broken back this way look like a "nest." In some instances broken fruit-bearing branches are also carried back to the security of the daybed.

Reproductive Behavior

Female spectacled bears begin to reproduce when around four years old. The breeding period is not well defined but usually occurs in the spring from April through June. In zoos, courtship and breeding behavior can last anywhere from one to five days. Gestation periods may vary between five and a half to eight months. Apparently, births are timed to coincide with the fruit season, usually about a month and a half before its peak. Because of these varying pregnancy lengths, scientists suspect delayed implantation, in which the fertilized ovum floats in the uterus for a period before implanting on a wall and continuing development. In particularly lean years, the embryos may be reabsorbed into the mother's body and no cubs will be born.

Births generally occur from November through February, with most occurring in January. Females den prior to giving birth to one or two (rarely three) cubs in a nest prepared on the ground under boulders or tree roots. (There is no evidence of hibernation in this species.) Birth weights usually range from 11 to 18 ounces (300 to 500 g). The cubs' eyes open in about twenty-five days and soon the cubs are out traveling with their mother. As they move about, the mother and cubs often communicate with a trilling sound, and the cubs may hum when nursing. An owl-like call has also been reported, and frightened spectacled bears may screech in alarm.

Sometimes an adult male accompanies a family group, but spectacled bears do not usually travel in pairs. Occasionally, the cubs will ride on their mother's back, especially if they become alarmed and are trying to escape. Individual cubs are also sometimes held against the mother's body with one paw as she runs on three legs. Mothers are reported to carry food to their cubs, which accompany their mother for six to eight months before striking out on their own.

A young spectacled bear rests on a high tree limb.

ASIAN BLACK BEARS:

Moon Bear in the Mountains

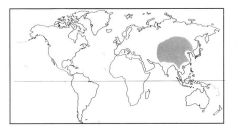

The Asian black bear's scientific name, *Selenarctos thibetanus*, literally means "moon bear of Tibet." Also called the Tibetan black bear and the Himalayan black bear, this sturdy and highly adaptable forest animal can be found from the bases of eastern Asia's coastal foothills up to 13,000 feet (4,000 m). It occurs in Iran, Afghanistan, and northern Pakistan, east through the Himalayas, as far south as Bangladesh and Laos, north throughout the Tibetan Plateau, Manchuria and other forested areas of China. Populations of Asian black bears are also found on Formosa (Taiwan) and the Japanese islands of Honshu and Shikoku. Until recently, it also occurred on the Japanese island of Kyushu.

DESCRIPTION OF THE MOON BEAR

It is called the moon bear because of the large, white crescent-shaped mark appearing on its chest. The rest of the body fur is jet black with a brown or tan muzzle and a whitish chin. The hair on the neck and shoulders forms a thick, long, manelike ruff. Individual bears living in the south, such as in eastern India's Assam hills, have shorter and thinner coats with less underwool (especially in winter) than those living at higher altitudes or in more northern regions. The ears are large and set rather far apart on their big, roundish heads. The short claws are very strong and quite useful in climbing trees.

The moon bear is medium sized, averaging 55 to 65 inches (140 to 165 cm) long. Average weights range from 200 to 255 pounds (90 to 115 kg). A large male may measure 77 inches (195 cm) long and weigh over 400 pounds (180 kg) when fat. Females normally are slightly smaller.

Sitting upright, an Asian black bear displays its crescent-shaped chest marking.

In Japan, Asian black bears often prefer mixed conifer and hardwood forests.

Earlier in this century, several subspecies of Asian black bears were described by naturalists. They included *Selenarctos thibetanus formosanus* of Formosa, *S.t. ussuricus* in Mongolia and the Ussuri region, and *S.t. japonicus* of Japan. It is very doubtful, however, that these represent true subspecies; they are most likely nothing more than geographic races of the same species. (See chapter 2 for a discussion on the races of the North American black bear.)

Recently, in the pristine and rugged Barun Valley of Nepal, an international team of researchers investigated reports of a new species of bear. Local hunters in this wet and remote region told stories of meeting two kinds of bears, one that lives on the ground *(bhui bhalu)* and another that lives and nests in the trees *(rukh bhalu)*. Although the villagers stubbornly asserted that these are really two different kinds of bears, the research team concluded, after examining various skulls, that the ground bear and the tree bear were one and the same species, the Asian black bear.

The researchers thought that the feeding habits of juvenile and adult Asian black bears in this region varied because of differing abilities to climb large trees in order to feed on nuts and fruits. (Heavy adults, especially males, lose some of their climbing ability.) The investigators theorized that a system has developed in which adults and juveniles have come to occupy different ecological niches—like a caterpiller and a butterfly, if you will. To my mind, the research was inconclusive, however. The ultimate proof would have been a chromosome and protein "fingerprint" made from the blood of several specimens. If these matched, we could be sure the villagers were just confusing two age groups of the same species.

FOOD HABITS OF THE MOON BEAR

Typically, the Asian black bear spends its day sleeping in a cave or hollow tree, coming out at dusk to seek food, but in some areas they are active during the day as well. In India and Tibet, these bears are carnivorous and often kill sheep, goats, and cattle. They are said to be able to take animals as large as adult buffalos by breaking their necks. Moon bears also eat termites, beetle larvae, honey, fruits, nuts, berries, and carrion. In the Indochina region they are frequently seen around villages, feeding on grain in the fields.

In Japan, because they are considered major economic pests, the food habits of these black bears have been extensively studied. Here, the moon bears subsist mostly on plant material throughout the year: In spring, they forage for beechnuts and oak nuts that fell the previous year and graze on fresh green shoots. In summer, they switch to wild cherries, dogwood, and ants and other insects, and during fall, they gorge and fatten for winter on the new crops of beechnuts and acorns.

This would be quite acceptable to the Japanese but Asian black bears (called Japanese black bears in Japan) also peel the bark from valuable timber trees, permanently damaging them and reducing their values. Bark peeling occurs mostly between mid-June and mid-July. After removing the bark from the base of a

In early spring, moon bears will forage for fallen acorns beneath oak trees.

A close-up of a moon bear nest, or enza, *made of broken branches.*

An enza *in a grove of Japanese red oaks.*

tree, the bears gnaw at the exposed sapwood. In districts where the forests have been transformed into one- or two-species tree plantations, the damage can have great economic impact. On some plantations, bears will debark as many as forty trees in a single night. Although seventeen conifer species are known to be affected, the most valuable timber species, Japanese cedar and Japanese cypress, seem to sustain the heaviest damage. In an attempt to reduce this problem, the bears are vigorously hunted—some 2,000 to 3,000 are killed annually as nuisances and for sport.

Another sign of feeding activity in Japan are treetop "bear's nests," colloquially known as *enza*. Resembling crows' nests, the structures are common in cherry, beech, oak, and dogwood trees. *Enza* are formed by the bear as it sits in a high fork, bending branches backward in order to reach its fruit. As broken branches accumulate around and under the bear, a kind of nest is formed. I have seen up to six or seven *enza* in a single oak grove. (Acorns are the moon bears' most important food in Japan.)

Asian black bears are also said to build "basking couches." These elevated, oval-shaped beds constructed of twigs and branches probably allow the bears to conserve body heat by getting off the ground during wet and cold spells. Some beds have been reported as high as 65 feet (20 m) in the tree, while others are only centimeters off the ground.

REPRODUCTION

Very little information is available about the reproductive behavior of this bear. The results of my zoo survey show that courtship and breeding in captivity usually take place during a one- or two-day period, often in May. Mating has been

witnessed as early as March and as late as December. In India, wild moon bears are said to mate in the autumn. Mock fights and "clucking" vocalizations sometimes occur during courtship.

The normal gestation period for this species varies between seven and eight months. Usually two (sometimes three) tiny cubs, weighing about 8 ounces (223 grams), are born in a cave or hollow tree during winter or early spring. The long pregnancy and the small size of the cubs are good indications that some sort of mechanism for delayed implantation is in operation. (See chapter 1 for a general discussion on delayed implantation.)

The cubs' eyes open in about a week, and within a month or two they are able to follow their mother as she forages. They remain with her from one to two years or until her next breeding cycle. Apparently, they may accompany their mother for even longer periods; females with two sets of cubs have been seen. Females may begin breeding at age three and have been known to live as long as thirty-three years in captivity.

Asian black bears have large, roundish heads and ears. Their nasty disposition is well known to the people living within the bear's habitat.

DENNING AND HIBERNATION

Asian black bears in the southern parts of their range may sleep for only short periods during the winter. Often they simply descend to a lower, warmer elevation where they can find food and remain active all winter. (However, pregnant females almost always den.) In colder and more northern regions, the cycle of hibernation behavior is well established. Hollow logs and trees are the bears' preferred denning sites, and they may remain asleep in them from November through late March or early April. In Japan, hibernating sites are nearly always located where deep snow will cover the den. According to Toshihiro Hazumi, one of Japan's few black-bear researchers, an insulating winter snow cover of more than 3 feet (1 m) is a key factor in the survival of Japanese moon bears.

STATUS AND FUTURE OF THE ASIAN BLACK BEAR

Wherever they occur, moon bears are constantly in trouble with humans. In addition to raids on domestic livestock and grain, there are numerous records of these bears mauling and killing people. An Indian forester described the bear to me as "a powerful beast of short temper." In Japan, during one bright April day in 1987, I was to experience a display of that temper.

I had joined Kazuhiko Maita, a black-bear researcher who was tracking fifteen radio-collared Asian black bears in the Akita district of northern Honshu. Although signs of spring were appearing in the mountains, two of his bears were still hibernating on a high, snow-covered slope. Mr. Maita had recently gained national attention in his country when several newspapers published photos he had made of a bear asleep in its den inside of a hollow tree. To make the pictures, he had blocked the bear's exit hole with a specially made iron grille and then drilled through the tree into the sleeping chamber. The bear's sleeping movements were recorded with the aid of a time-lapse camera. I was invited to accompany Maita's team as they attempted to set up an observation post at one of the two remaining occupied dens.

After three hours of climbing through deep snow, we arrived at the den site. Since I was much larger and heavier than anyone else in the party, I kept breaking through the snow crust and so was the last in line. The bear was inside a fallen tree trunk that lay on the ground at a 45-degree angle. By using a radio locater to pinpoint the exact position of the bear, we calculated that it was asleep some 10 feet (3 m) or so from an entrance at the high end of the log. While Maita's team of graduate students prepared their equipment in order to block the den's entrance, I searched for a patch of snow that would support my weight and began to set up a camera on a tripod. Guns are severely restricted in Japan, so no one in our team was armed. I did, however, have a spray can of a recently developed chemical bear deterrent in my back pocket. It probably saved my life.

As Maita's team cautiously approached the den entrance with their equipment, a very large (485 pound/220 kg) male Asian black bear exploded from the entrance in attack. The team dropped everything and scattered, but the bear had singled out one of the graduate students who had fallen through the snow crust while trying to escape. In a moment the bear closed in on him. That was when I sprayed the animal with a blast from my can of deterrent. The graduate student scampered away, and the bear immediately turned on me, face to face. I hit him with another blast of spray. This time the bear wheeled and ran down the mountain and out of sight.

We were shaken but unharmed. Mr. Maita's first words after the attack were, "I must have that spray. . . . I *must* have that spray!" Earlier, he had

Kazuhiko Maita adjusts his array of telemetry equipment that he uses to monitor two radio-collared hibernating moon bears in northern Honshu.

Top right: Maita and a graduate student cautiously approach the den of a hibernating Asian black bear.

Bottom right: Moments later, the bear suddenly appears and charges.

The scene of the scuffle; the attacking bear was repelled by a chemical spray containing red pepper oil. The red stains are not blood, but a marking dye used in the spray.

scoffed at the idea that my little can of repellent might be able to protect us. (A complete discussion on personal safety and bear deterrents can be found in chapter 9.)

This was the first time Maita's research group had ever been attacked by a bear. We had rudely awakened him from his winter's sleep, and this species' short temper makes them especially dangerous. Each year in Japan, two or three people are killed and another ten to twenty are injured by bears. The worst month for attacks is June, when people collect wild bamboo shoots in the forest. Since the bears also like bamboo shoots, confrontations are inevitable. (In 1986, because of a failure of the acorn crop, the casualty list was doubled because bears seeking food had been forced into areas more frequented by humans.)

Because the moon bear is greatly feared, legal protection in all parts of its range is poorly enforced or simply nonexistent. Although a hunting season has been established, Japanese bears are considered a verminous species, and trapping and killing them are encouraged by the government. At the present rate of hunting (and habitat destruction), the moon bear may have only about ten to twenty years of existence left in that country. Japan has no preserves or conservation plans for bears. They are hunted even inside the national parks.

The moon bear's continued survival in the Himalayan region is jeopardized because the Chinese believe its meat, bile, and bones have medicinal properties. Also, its paws are relished as a food delicacy. One day in a marketplace in Chengdu, China, Mark Newman and I counted bear parts and skeletons. In less than an hour we found a total of 168 dead moon bears.

In India, a different kind of hunting threatens the moon bear. After their mothers are shot, young cubs are captured, muzzled, and trained to ride bicycles, walk upright, and "dance" by itinerant street performers and circuses. (Asian black bears are very bipedal and have been known to walk upright for over a quarter of a mile (.4 km) on their hind legs.) India's wildlife department claims to be taking steps to curb this activity, but it is difficult, they say, because performing bears are the sole livelihood of some people and local politicians bow to pressure not to crack down on the practice.

Because of its fearsome reputation and great economic value for food and medicine, it does not seem that any serious conservation effort for the Asian black bear will occur until its numbers become so severely depleted that the species is critically endangered.

In India, China, and other parts of southeast Asia, captive moon bears are trained to perform in circuses and roadside shows. The most bipedal of all bears, moon bears have been known to walk upright for over a quarter of a mile (.4 km).

Combining its natural intelligence and agility, this bear has been trained to pedal and steer a bicycle unaided.

If conservation plans are not implented, soon the only moon bears remaining may be those in zoos.

GIANT PANDAS:

The Bamboo Bear

Few animals have stirred the public's imagination more than this endearing roly-poly black-and-white bear. These deadpan clowns are China's national treasure and have become the World Wildlife Fund's symbol of conservation. Around the world, children of all ages adore millions of stuffed and inflatable toys made in this animal's image. However, although the panda is a familiar figure to nearly everyone, only recently have we unlocked the secrets of this shy animal's life in the wild.

THE BODY OF THE PANDA

The giant panda *(Ailuropoda melanoleauca)* resembles other bears in its general shape and body proportions. Its basic color is white with black eye patches, ears, legs, feet, chest, and shoulders. Sometimes the very tip of its 5-inch (13-cm)-long tail is also black. In the forest, this black-and-white pattern makes the animal very conspicuous at close range, but on snow it practically vanishes. (Early in 1986, a light-brown color phase of the giant panda was discovered.) Panda fur is thick, with coarse outer hairs and extremely dense and woolly underfur that becomes somewhat sparse on the belly. Cubs are as soft to the touch as kittens.

Adult pandas range between 5.25 and 6 feet (160 to 180 cm) in length and may attain weights of well over 200 pounds (91 kg). Males and females are identically marked, but adult males usually weigh from 10 to 20 percent more than females. The Chinese name for the giant panda is *xiongmao,* or "giant cat bear," the pupils of the panda's eyes are catlike vertical slits. All other bears have round pupils.

The giant panda is probably the most loved and most endangered bear in the world.

Lying on its back, a roly-poly panda uses a hind foot to scratch an itch. The panda's famous "thumb" can be seen on its outstretched forepaw.

A panda's forepaws are very flexible and are equipped with a peculiar sixth digit that works something like an opposable thumb. The evolution of this "thumb" has been a subject of debate for over 100 years. In reality, the thumb is only an enlarged wrist bone (the radial sesamoid) that is capable of independent movement. It is very important to the panda, however, because it allows it to handle bamboo stems and leaves (the panda's major food) with great precision and dexterity. The panda's hind feet lack the heel pad found on other bears'. Their clumsy-looking, pigeon-toed walk is misleading, because pandas are able to move with remarkable ease and silence through the densest forest and roughest terrain.

Because pandas must chew tough bamboo stalks for nourishment, they have massive skulls equipped with large, crushing molars. Powerful muscles attached to a prominent sagittal crest (a ridge of bone on top of the skull) move the jaws. For protection from sharp bamboo splinters, the esophagus has a tough, horny lining and the stomach is almost gizzardlike in its thick-walled, muscular construction. The rest of the digestive system, very similar to that of a typical carnivore, is inefficient in its handling and digestion of bamboo. Consequently, the animal must consume up to 45 pounds (20 kg) of the plant a day to survive.

HISTORICAL AND PREHISTORICAL PANDAS

Apparently, giant pandas appeared during the Pliocene epoch, somewhere between 3 to 12 million years ago. At that time they roamed over much of eastern China, as far north as Beijing and as far south as northern Burma. Three fossil forms of giant pandas have been described, but only one, *Ailuropoda microta*, was significantly different from the species we know—it was about half the size of the present-day panda.

Chinese books written more than 3,000 years ago mention this lumbering black-and-white animal: Poet Bai Juyi (772–846) credited the panda with mystic powers capable of preventing pestilence and exorcising evil spirits. Perhaps it was because of these alleged virtues that panda skulls were included among the burial objects in the tomb of an ancient Chinese nobleman that was unearthed in 1956 near Xi'an. For centuries panda pelts were considered royal gifts. Now that the animal is regarded as a priceless heritage, the present of a live panda is China's highest gesture of friendship. This universally loved animal provides a link between East and West that transcends all political differences.

The first Westerner to discover the panda was Père Armand David, a French explorer and priest who, in 1868, was shown two female specimens shot by his Chinese hunters. A year later, the panda pelts and skins sent home by Father David astonished the learned scientists of Europe and America. Several panda-hunting expeditions were immediately launched, but it wasn't until 1929 that the first Westerner shot a panda. (By most accounts, Theodore Roosevelt takes credit for this dubious honor.) For the next seven years, numerous collection expeditions combed China in search of live specimens, without much success.

Then, in 1936, Ruth Harkness, whose husband was killed during a panda expedition, arrived in Chicago with the first live panda to reach the West. America immediately fell in love with it. What a time Ruth must have had showing off her prize! The cub, named Su-Lin, was acquired by the Chicago Zoological Park the following year. According to Kenneth Johnson, a biologist with the World Wildlife Fund/China Giant Panda Project, by 1949 (the year of the Chinese Communist Revolution) seventy-three pandas had left China, and many others had been killed by hunters.

The giant panda resembles other bears in its general shape and body proportions. In the forest, its black-and-white markings are very conspicuous at close range, but on snow they practically vanish.

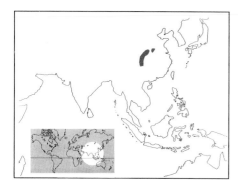

THE PANDA'S DWINDLING RANGE AND NUMBERS

Hunting and habitat destruction have eliminated pandas from most of their former range. Today, they exist only in six small areas along the eastern rim of the Tibetan Plateau, in a cold, damp coniferous forest between 4,000 and 11,000 feet (1,200 to 3,400 m) high. The bamboo that the pandas depend on for food is found mostly within this narrow band. However, footprints and droppings have been recorded as high as 13,250 feet (4,040 m). Although the panda's total range encompasses some 11,300 square miles (29,500 sq km), George Shaller, a pioneering researcher for the WWF/China Giant Panda Project, estimates that probably less than 20 percent, or 2,250 square miles (5,900 sq km), represents actual panda habitat. More than half the pandas remaining in the wild live in a chain of twelve reserves established by the Chinese. According to a recent census conducted by China's Ministry of Forestry and the World Wildlife Fund, the wild panda population has declined by about 200 in the last decade, to an estimated 700. Several colonies have disappeared altogether, and others have been reduced to fewer than 20 pandas, which is considered too small to remain viable. Another 120 pandas or so survive in zoos, mostly in China.

Right: The mountains in China's Wolong preserve are some of the last remaining panda habitat.

A closed-canopy forest with a bamboo understory seems to be the giant panda's preferred habitat.

THE CLASSIFICATION CONTROVERSY

When Père David first described the panda, he thought it was a new kind of bear, and he gave it the scientific name *Ursus melanoleucas*. Most Western scientists agreed, until they got their first view of a living panda in 1936. Then they began to have doubts; it certainly looked bearish, but there were all those unique features—its bamboo diet, its black eye patches, and its hazy ancestral line—to

consider. True bears are more carnivorous, it was argued, and unlike other bears, pandas do not hibernate or roar. (They bleat instead.) The learned gentlemen finally concluded that the giant panda must be a genealogical relative to the much smaller red or lesser panda *(Ailurus fulgens),* which was thought to be related to the raccoon. The red panda, known since 1821, looks remarkably like a raccoon, and like the giant panda, it eats bamboo. The giant panda was quickly shifted from the bear genus, *Ursus,* to *Ailuropoda* and eventually the two pandas came to share, somewhat uncomfortably, an order all their own. Not everyone was convinced; a few naturalists still considered the giant panda to be a kind of bear.

The first proof came in 1964, when D. Dwight Davis published his great comparative anatomy work, *The Giant Panda: A Morphological Study of Evolutionary Mechanisms.* His thorough and painstaking work debunked the giant panda's tie to raccoons. Its confusing similarities to the red panda were the results of parallel evolution toward a common function. "Every morphological feature examined indicates that the giant panda is nothing more than a highly specialized bear," he concluded.

Biology's taxonomic foundations had been shaken, but a few skeptics remained unconvinced. Then along came the genetic research. During a two-year effort, geneticist Stephen O'Brien and his team of scientists from the National Cancer Institute and the National Zoological Park slowly pieced together the true relationship between bears, pandas, and raccoons. They examined cell-culture material and blood samples from each species in order to compare DNA sequences, protein characteristics, and chromosomes. In all, the proof included four independent tests using the latest methods of molecular biology. The announcement of their findings were published in the September 12–18, 1985, issue of *Nature:* Giant pandas really are bears after all. And what about the red panda? The chromosomes say they're related to raccoons. Between 20 to 40 million years ago, there was a split from a common ancestor. One line led to the bears, the other to the raccoons and red pandas. Giant pandas, because they have specialized in eating bamboo, have slowly drifted away from the rest of the bears' family tree.

FOOD AND FEEDING HABITS

The giant panda's diet has also been a controversy since their discovery. Although they eat bamboo almost exclusively, pandas will eat meat if given an opportunity. They are too slow to catch most animals, but they have been reported to eat fish, pikas, and rodents and even to enter logging camps in order to steal meat. All captive pandas will eat meat, and most zoos include at least meat powder and milk as dietary supplements. Giant pandas will also eat crocuses, irises, vines, horsetails, fir bark, and certain kinds of tufted grass. Some local people claim that these animals will also raid beehives for honey.

One clever hunting strategy used by pandas to catch bamboo rats *(Rhizomys sinense)* was described to us by our Chinese hosts at the Wolong Panda Reserve. If a giant panda finds a promising bamboo rat burrow, it stomps on the shallow ground above and around the burrow's entrance. When the frightened rat runs out, the panda catches it in its mouth.

Anatomically, the panda's carnivore-like digestive system seems best suited for digesting meat. But in the cold forests of the panda's winter home, easy prey is extremely scarce. Only bamboo provides a ready food source of fresh leaves and stems throughout the year.

When eating, giant pandas usually sit upright.

Usually the panda feeds sitting upright, a position that allows the forelegs to manipulate bamboo stalks. This is where that famous radial sesamoid "thumb" comes into play. George Schaller, who has done considerable panda watching, describes the actions of one of his study animals: "Sitting, he bends the bamboo toward his mouth, biting the tops off last year's shoots and leaves off stems; moving a few feet he then eats some more, munching a swath through his domain. Once he ate from 3,481 stems in the course of one day."

Larger stems are quickly peeled with a series of bites into the tough outer layers, accompanied by jerks of the head. The peeled stem is then fed into the mouth, to be chewed a section at a time. (Approximately 6.7 chews per mouthful.) Within a few minutes a large pile of bamboo peelings can accumulate in a panda's lap. When satiated, pandas often lie back and take a nap. Because they are unable to process bamboo efficiently, most of it will pass undigested in a few hours. Leaving behind a copious fifteen to twenty pounds of spindle-shaped droppings, the panda then resumes its feeding. George Schaller's team calculated that a panda digests only about 17 percent of the food it eats. (For a typical herbivore, the figure is around 80 percent.) "Though a panda may spend two-thirds of the day eating," Schaller writes, "it obtains at best only a small surplus of calories beyond those it needs for body maintenance and growth."

Bamboo leaves contain the greatest level of digestible protein (around 16 percent), and it's amazingly consistent throughout the year. However, for some reason, the leaves are not eaten during the spring. Perhaps high silica levels make them unpalatable at that time, Schaller suggests. In spring, some pandas drop to lower altitudes in order to feast on new bamboo shoots. As much as 84 pounds (38 kg) of shoots (around 45 percent of the total body weight) may be eaten in a single day. Altogether, over fifteen species of bamboo are eaten, with different parts of the plants favored at different seasons.

The bamboo that is so abundant over the panda's range is usually an extremely reliable food source. Normally, bamboo reproduces each year by sending up new shoots from underground stems. But every 40 to 120 years, depending on the species, all members of bamboo species in a given area will simultaneously flower, seed, and then die en masse. In the past, this synchronous flowering may actually have benefited the panda. Giant pandas are very conservative about migrating, preferring to live their lives within a small area.

Because the bears are unable to digest bamboo efficiently, most of its bulk will pass through the animals in a few hours. After resting, giant pandas may leave behind fifteen or twenty pounds (7 to 9 kg) of spindle-shaped droppings.

Bamboo leaves contain the highest level of digestible protein. Bamboo grows so abundantly that it has become the panda's most reliable and preferred food.

With so little mixing of populations, pandas eventually run the risk of inbreeding problems. When the bamboo dies off, pandas are forced to move to new areas, thus mixing the gene pool. Usually there are several species of bamboo distributed on an elevation gradient across a mountain, providing an alternate food source. However, if a panda's range contains only one or two species of bamboo when this happens, the bear may be in for serious trouble. In the mid-1970s and again in 1983, much of the arrow and umbrella bamboo (two species that the panda prefers) in northern Sichuan province flowered and died. Chinese scientists reported that at least 138 bears—perhaps as much as one-quarter of the panda population—starved to death. New bamboo seedlings take as long as 10 or 15 years to grow large enough to become good panda food. Moreover, today's pandas have nowhere to go. Farming and villages have cut the panda's habitat into widely separated mountaintop "islands" containing only a single species of bamboo.

SOCIAL AND OTHER BEHAVIORS

Bamboo thickets provide pandas not only with food but also with protective cover in which they carry out their secluded lives. Built both short and squat, they slip through the densest undergrowth with incredible ease. Pandas often move in a kind of studied and restrained way, apparently in order to conserve energy; when not feeding, they often just lie around like cats. Only when startled can they be induced to flee in a trot (instead of galloping like other bears). Pandas may sometimes stand erect, but they never walk in this position. They frequently climb trees, descending rump first. They are also known to mark trees with claw scratches.

It is well the giant panda conserves its energy. On its low-energy diet of bamboo, it is impossible to accumulate enough fat to be able to hibernate through the winter. Instead of hibernating, pandas descend to lower elevations where they can continue to feed. Although pandas do not make winter dens, they will occasionally take shelter in a hollow tree or rock crevice during a particularly fierce snowstorm. Wild pandas are most active around dawn and early evening, but periodic activity occurs throughout the day and night (roughly about 60 percent of each 24-hour period), most of it being devoted to feeding.

No one knows how long a giant panda may live in the wild, but in captivity they have been known to live thirty years. Once in a while, cubs and very old individuals fall victim to wild dogs or leopards, but adult pandas have very few enemies other than humans. The most common natural problems bothering wild pandas are ailments: roundworms, indigestion, and lung disease.

Panda home ranges are small, varying from 1.5 to 2.5 square miles (3.8 to 6.5 sq km), and are normally shared with other pandas. In his classic book *The Giant Pandas of Wolong* George Schaller describes the panda's home range:

> A panda population consists of several residents, each living within a small stable home range, all or part of which is shared with others. Adult males and females, however, appear to have somewhat different land tenure systems. Females are well dispersed. Although their ranges may overlap, each female spends most of her time within a discrete core area only 30 to 40 hectares [75 to 100 acres] in extent. . . . Males occupy greatly overlapping ranges and lack well-defined core areas, spending time within the core areas of females and subadults.

Far left: Relaxing in a doorway, a giant panda at China's Chongqing Zoo sleepily digests a heavy meal of bamboo.

Clownish even when at ease, giant pandas have only recently been bred successfully outside of China.

Though they share ranges, pandas try to avoid one another. "They are alone together," Schaller writes. "Meetings are a blend of coolness and violence and remarkably noisy—a medly of squeals, yips, chirps, moans, and barks." Apparently, interactions are based on rank rather than territorial priority. Face-to-face encounters actually are rather rare, though.

The self-contained panda is usually kept informed of others in the neighborhood by an efficient network of scent stations along primary travel routes. (Usually quite sedentary, pandas occasionally get the urge to travel, sometimes as far as 2.5 miles (4 km) in a single day.) Scent stations are often located at the bases of large conifer trees or other prominent sites such as ridges or boulders. Pandas have several scent glands near the anus whose products are smeared on the scent stations with the aid of that brushlike tail. Sprayed urine is also used as a marker. (I have watched male pandas in zoos practically do handstands in their effort to urinate high on a wall.) Both sexes use scent marking, but it is more common among males.

Pandas seem to be very intelligent and are capable of being highly trained. In captivity, pandas at the Fuzhou Zoo in China have been taught to do more than twenty stunts, including riding a bicycle, rolling somersaults, eating with a knife and fork, and dunking a basketball. They have also been trained to submit placidly to medical tests and treatment without the use of force or anesthesia. Pairs of these stunt-performing pandas are sometimes leased to other zoos around the world.

PANDA REPRODUCTION

Giant pandas reproduce very slowly, and infant mortality is high. Growth is slow; they may not reach sexual maturity until they are from five to seven years old. The mating season generally runs from mid-March into May. During this time, up to four or five males will surround and compete for a female who is in heat. Priority is often based on rank. When mating, the female assumes a crouching, head-down position as the male mounts. (Incidentally, the panda's baculum (penis bone) is quite different from that of any other carnivore; it's short and rodlike, with winglike expansions.) Actual copulation time is short, varying from only 30 seconds to five minutes, but the male may mount repeatedly. One researcher witnessed forty-eight copulations in the space of three hours. Mating is also a very noisy time, accompanied by much moaning and squealing. A second estrus may occur in late fall.

The gestation period ranges from 3.5 to 5.5 months. Because newborn pandas are so tiny (only 3 to 5 ounces (90 to 140 g)), there appears to be a delay of embryo implantation and development for several months. The mother panda usually gives birth in a cave or hollow tree in late August or September. The blind, toothless 6-inch-long newborn cubs are pink, almost naked, and helpless. They have a surprisingly loud cry that can be heard over 100 yards (90 m) away. Although the mother often gives birth to two cubs, she soon abandons one without any attempt to take care of it, and the abandoned cub soon dies. According to Schaller, the birth of the second cub is little more than insurance in case the first cub is not viable. "To hold, suckle, and carry two helpless young for four or five months until they are mobile is probably too difficult," he writes.

The mother panda cradles her baby in her forepaws almost continuously for the first three weeks of its life. She usually sits upright and holds her baby to her breast for suckling very much like a human mother nursing a child. She will lavish an amazing amount of care and attention on her cub; she even puts a paw under her chin for safety when carrying the cub in her mouth.

Black fur begins to appear in the second week, and adult coloration is attained by the end of the first month or so. The cub's eyes open around six weeks of age. The den is used for about six weeks, and from then on the cub is carried by the mother until it can walk. The baby panda's legs are very weak at birth, and it is nearly two and a half months before it can even stand up; by the middle of the fourth month, though, the cub can finally run and play. Panda cubs begin eating bamboo around five or six months of age and by nine months are fully weaned. By the time they are one year old, they weigh about 75 pounds (35 kg). Pandas usually leave their mothers when around one and a half years old. At best, female pandas can rear only one cub every two years; usually the rate is lower.

CURRENT STATUS AND EFFORTS AT CONSERVATION

The giant panda is an endangered species with a bleak future. Only 700 or so still exist in the wild. Like most other endangered species, pandas are victims of the inexorable expansion of human civilization; removal of the forest canopy by loggers and farmers has become one of the most serious threats to the panda's existence. Satellite photographs of panda habitats during the last decade show a direct correlation between loss of forest habitats and the decline of pandas. Pandas prefer to forage in bamboo thickets that are in the shelter of tall trees. As the trees are harvested, the pandas seek new habitats. But now there are few places left for them to go.

Even more serious than the shrinking size of the habitat is the increasing genetic isolation of pandas trapped in small populations by deforested areas and farms. Most panda communities have fewer than twenty individuals. When the number of animals in an isolated community is this low, they become especially vulnerable to chance events and inbreeding. A whole new generation could be born all male, or the few adult breeders could be killed by poachers. If the situation is not reversed quickly, pandas may be completely gone from the wild by the year 2000.

Serious efforts to save the giant panda were launched in 1957. By 1978 China had set aside a dozen panda reserves totaling nearly 2,300 square miles (6,000 sq km). In cooperation with the World Wildlife Fund, a state-run research center complete with laboratories, breeding enclosures, and nurseries was built in Wolong, the largest reserve. Located in the western mountains of Sichuan Province, Wolong is 770 square miles (2,000 sq km) of extremely rugged terrain, about half above timberline and unsuitable for pandas. A hundred or more still roam the narrow belt of forest sandwiched between alpine ice and the busy farms below.

When Mark Newman and I tried to visit Wolong, we were in for frustrating times filled with many delays. We got as close as Chengdu, a day's drive to the reserve, but were then held up by numerous and conflicting bureaucratic excuses. Each time we applied for permission we heard a different story—"No foreign visitors allowed" or "Need special visa." For us, moving through China was like trying to force one's way through cold molasses: The substance yields

At the May First field center in Wo-long, Mark Newman chats with the station's research staff.

under steady pressure, but one still makes very little headway. Finally, in desperation, I threatened to file a bad report. "Bad report?!" We were on our way to Wolong the next day.

Wolong reminded me of the mountains near my home in Washington State: cool, misty evergreen forests sprinkled with waterfalls and hardwood trees. After six weeks of traveling through teeming cities we had finally arrived at the panda's home. An entry from my journal describes my first real view:

> Standing on top of a rock overlook at an altitude of 8,500 feet [2,600 m], I look across this forested stream valley toward a mist-shrouded mountain—the most peaceful spot I have found in all of China. At some dim time in prehistory, perhaps the whole country was this way. Now only these mountaintop islands, anchored in a sea of mankind, survive. But even here, my reverie is short lived. My Chinese mountain guide is so eager to get back to camp that he is becoming a nuisance; he doesn't want to miss even a single meal. At the far end of the valley, the mist has cleared just enough for me to see that the neighboring mountains, terraced three-quarters of the way to their tops with farms, are practically denuded of forest. Somewhere below me, moving like wraiths through the bamboo jungle, are three pandas—all wearing radio collars. I know they are near, we can hear their radio voices clicking in the receiver headset.

At Wolong, radio-collared pandas are tracked with directional antennas.

Right: Visitors at the Chengdu Zoo in China tempt a panda with choice bamboo stalks and leaves.

Local villagers are not the only people who share Wolong's landscape. Within its bounderies, a town of 350 people staff and administer the preserve. Here, administrators talked about relocating the mountain farm communities, setting up travel corridors between panda populations, and replanting the forest with several species of bamboo. But, so far, progress has been as about as elusive as the panda. A complex of apartment buildings, built to house villagers relocated from the upper valleys, stood empty, their windows broken by mischievous children. Farmers are reluctant to give up their comfortable wood-and-rock homes and move into these small, concrete apartments—even if they are provided free of charge. These independent mountain people cling to their traditional lifestyle, passed down through innumerable generations.

Farther down the valley, seven species of bamboo grow in well-tended nurseries. It is a hopeful sign, but efforts at replanting a variety of bamboo species in the wild has not been very successful. Until recently, the government was lax

Above: Lightly restrained, a giant panda receives veterinary attention at the Chengdu Zoo.

Right: Terrace farming has all but denuded many of the mountains surrounding the villages in Wolong preserve.

Bottom: A cooperative effort between the World Wildlife Fund and China has resulted in the creation of a panda breeding and research facility at Wolong.

Far right: Each panda in Wolong's breeding facility has its own front yard. At night, free-ranging pandas sometimes come down from the mountains for a visit.

A Chinese zookeeper proudly shows off the results of their successful panda-breeding program.

In Tokyo, long lines greet each day's opening of the panda exhibit at the zoo. Zoo employees armed with megaphones keep the line moving.

in controlling local hunters. Snares set out to catch musk deer often kill pandas. So do spear traps set out for takin, a kind of large antelope. According to George Schaller, snares are the second biggest cause of panda deaths, after habitat destruction. Poachers would receive a two-year jail sentence if convicted. Few, if any, ever have been.

The Chinese have a saying "If an animal moves with its back to the sky, then it is edible." Practically anything that moves, then, is eaten or used for medicinal purposes. Theoretically nearly all hunting is illegal in China, yet in a single marketplace in Chengdu, we were sickened to see the carcasses of over 150 bears, several snow leopards and clouded leopards, a tiger, 5 endangered red pandas and hundreds of monkeys and smaller animals. Yet there are signs that China has begun to clamp down on animal poaching. In October of 1987, Chinese authorities decided to impose the death penalty on anyone convicted of killing giant pandas or smuggling their skins. This is the strictest antipoaching law in the world.

If efforts to save the wild panda fail, it still may be possible to prolong the species through artificial insemination. For a long time, breeding in captivity was thought to be impossible, but in 1963 the Beijing Zoo surprised the world with its first panda birth. In 1978, the same zoo delivered the first artificially conceived cub. Today, most captive panda births are the products of artificial insemination. Though many cubs have died, more than fifty litters have now been born in captivity. China's Chengdu Zoo, a leader in this kind of research, has now established a success rate of better than 70 percent. Pandas are the most sought-after zoo animal in the world. Outside China, there are only eight zoos that have permanently residing pandas. The biggest problem to overcome has been determining exactly when a female is ready to ovulate. (There are very few hours in the year when a panda can become pregnant.) After artificial insemination, the mother-to-be is allowed to mate naturally with a male. If the procedure is successful, expectant mothers are placed in wooden-floored nesting rooms and given a special diet. After delivery, the babies are hand-raised by attendants.

The public is so entranced by these black-and-white bears that when the female panda (Ling-Ling) at the National Zoo in Washington, D.C., becomes ill, she receives thousands of get-well cards. Every year, schoolchildren from all over the United States send valentines to Ling Ling and her mate, Hsing Hsing. When Tokyo's Ueno Zoo had a panda birth in 1986, more than 270,000 people suggested names for the little cub. When the zoo finally allowed a public viewing, nearly 13,000 people stood in line for a glimpse and another 200,000 called the "Dial-a-Panda" hot line each day to hear him squealing. When I visited Tokyo's zoo six months later, the weekend lineup was still several city blocks long. Prompters with megaphones were yelling at the crowd to keep people moving quickly through the exhibit. Knots of curious viewers jostled each other to get a peek at live TV coverage of the cub on monitors set up all over the zoo's grounds. The scene was the embodiment of "pandamania," a term coined by the media to describe how these animals affect people. I hope the giant panda will always be with us.

LIVING WITH BEARS:

History Lessons for the Future

F rom prehistory to the present, human beings have had a continual but varying relationship with bears. In this chapter we take a look at attitudes and problems, past and present, and then try to peer ahead into the possible future for bears in our world.

BEARS IN ANCIENT CULTURES

Bears and people have been influencing one another for a long time. Seventy-five thousand years ago, Stone Age hunters stood in awe of these powerful beasts, yet they somehow managed to kill thousands of the animals. Armed at first with only spears and stone axes, some of these hunters must have performed feats of extreme courage. Preparing spiritually as well as physically for these tasks, many hunting cultures developed religious traditions that deified the bear. To overcome the animal's great power, each hunter prayed that the bear's spirit would forgive him for killing it. Ceremonial dances and songs, still performed today in many tribal groups, were designed to help placate the mysterious powers controlling the success or failure of the hunt. Through these religious traditions, bears became honored deities around the world.

Bears' humanlike attributes allow people to feel a close kinship with them. In North America some Indian tribes referred to bears as their grandfathers, grandmothers, cousins, and brothers. Believing them to be reincarnated family members, a few tribes refused to kill bears at all. Wherever prehistoric people lived near bears, legends arose about bears who could turn into people or people who turned into bears that could speak and teach children the wisdom of the

An Alaskan brown bear family uses a rock outcropping as a convenient overlook. Bears will often use prominent places to monitor the surrounding country.

forest. All over the Northern Hemisphere, from the Swiss Alps, across Siberia, in Japan and Korea, through Alaska and the rest of North America, these old legends have some remarkable similarities.

"One idea that was repeated over and over is the bear as the symbol of death and rebirth," says David Rockwell, a Montana naturalist who has done extensive comparative research into ancient bear cults. In hibernation, the bear was believed to die every fall and then be reborn in the spring. "The bear figures strongly in a lot of puberty rites simply because it fits the initiatory pattern so well."

Typically, the candidate for adulthood was isolated from his or her family and sent into the forest to sit in a tiny hut resembling a bear's den. The hut was dark and there the initiate had to sit alone, fasting or meditating for a certain period before being allowed to return to the community as a reborn person. Almost every northern tribe and culture had its own variation on this basic theme.

One of the more elaborate initiations for example, was the North American Dakota Indian puberty rite for boys, called "making a bear." "The boy had a dream that told him it was time for him to go through the ceremony," Rockwell explains.

So the tribe prepared a ceremonial ground that included a pole erected with a piece of buckskin hanging from it, and on the buckskin were images from the boy's dream. The boy spent maybe two or three days fasting and sitting around that pole, and then about 100 yards [90m] away the boy dug a hole into the ground. This was called the "bear's hole." Ditches, called "entrances to the bear's hole" were made across the pit in the four directions. The boy then spent up to four days in the hole, fasting and imitating a bear.

On the last day, the young men from his village would gather around and provoke the "bear" from his den, who would charge out and fight. The young men would try to symbolically kill him with knives or with guns loaded with only powder. After wrestling around for a while, the "bear" would escape and go back to the den. Then the "hunters" would charge in on another entrance and the "bear" would come out again. This went on through all four entrances. At the last entrance the "bear" would really try to escape because at that point he could not return to the den. He would either escape to the woods, where he would remain all day or, more often, be symbolically killed and carried like a corpse to a lodge, where he sat with an assistant and smoked and prayed for the rest of the day. At the end, he issued from the lodge, reborn as a man.

EUROPEANS AND BEARS

To the ancient Romans, the bear was simply a symbol of brute strength. For hundreds of years after the Roman legions first penetrated the forests beyond the Alps, Germanic and other European tribes exported bears south, back to Rome. Some Roman emperors kept them as pets in their menageries, other used them for sport. In the arena, bears were pitted by thrill-seeking Romans against dogs and gladiators in bloody spectacles. The Emperor Caligula (until A.D. 41) once used 400 bears in a single day, and Emperor Gordian (until A.D. 238) was said to have used nearly 1,000 bears in one grand and gory extravaganza.

In the Dark Ages, when commerce between Europe and the rest of the world was at an ebb, the bear was practically the only large predator that Europeans could obtain. Consequently, it took the place of the lion and tiger in the collections of wealthy princes. In England, the lordly sport of bearbaiting grew to be such a popular amusement that it endured as a holiday entertainment from the time of the Norman Conquest well into the eighteenth century. The sport was simple to arrange; a bear was chained to a stake by its neck or by a hind leg and then was worried by a pack of vicious dogs. It is said that thirteen bears were used in a spectacle of this kind staged for the benefit of Elizabeth I, the queen of England. The event was described by one writer as a very pleasant time. "The bear tore after the dogs, and when bitten by them would bite, claw, and roar, and nimbly tumble himself free of them. When he was loose he would shake himself with blood and slaver hanging about." Perhaps the royal lady was pleased and edified, but bearbaiting was an absolute horror to the Puritans. They tried to prohibit it, with only partial success—not because of the pain it gave to the bears but because of the pleasure it gave to the spectators.

For centuries bears have been popular subjects for training and performance. During the eighteenth and nineteenth centuries, hundreds of itinerant showmen exhibited trained bears from village to village throughout Europe. Usually two showmen accompanied each bear, one playing a violin or tamborine while the other put the animal through its routine. The bears were dressed in burlesque costumes, and their antics were extremely popular. Some mountain villagers made their living by capturing bear cubs for this circus trade. There were even "bear academies," where the animals were taught tricks. But the training was often conducted with such cruelty that bear circuses in Russia were finally prohibited in 1867. Trained bears are still popular in many parts of Asia, however, and are occasionally even seen in Europe and America.

The Bear in the American Mind

The special status accorded the bear by the American Indians was rudely brushed aside by the European pioneers. Though they valued bear meat and hides, most settlers considered the living animal as little more than a nuisance that interfered with farming and livestock raising. As civilization spread westward, the number of bears declined drastically. By the end of the nineteenth century, black bear populations in the eastern third of the United States had reached their lowest levels. Grizzlies had been removed from the prairies and now were found only in secluded mountains. Through year-round hunting, trapping, and poisoning, the "varmints" had been all but eliminated.

The first break for the bear came in 1902, when President Theodore Roosevelt, while on a hunting trip, refused to shoot a black bear chained to a tree. The incident seized the public's imagination, and toy bears were created to celebrate the event. This is how the popular teddy bear came to be. From that point on, nearly all of us has had a teddy bear at one time in our life, and that association seems to have helped soften our view toward the verminous bear.

World War II also provided another great boost for the bear's image. After a Japanese submarine shelled the southern California coast, forestry officials feared that future attacks might start widespread forest fires along America's West Coast, and so they organized a cooperative forest-fire prevention campaign. At first, during 1942 and 1943, only wartime slogans were used. Then, in 1944, Walt Disney's Bambi was featured on a poster. This proved so successful that the

Wartime Advertising Council and the Forest Service decided to create their own animal to represent forest fire prevention. "Smokey the Bear" was born, named after "Smokey Joe" Martin, who was assistant chief of the New York City Fire Department from 1919 to 1930. After the war, the Wartime Advertising Council, renamed the Advertising Council, continued to use "Smokey" in their public service campaigns. By the 1950s, "Smokey the Bear" had become so well known that Congress saw fit to pass the Smokey Bear Act in order to protect his image by law. Today, the bear in the wide-brimmed hat is a familiar friend to everyone.

The first living Smokey the Bear was found in 1950 after a forest fire had devastated the Lincoln National Forest in New Mexico. When the flames had died and the smoke cleared, the only living thing the fire fighters saw was a badly burned bear cub clinging to a blackened tree. The little cub was taken to a ranger station and nursed back to health. They called the cub "Smokey" after the poster bear, and after his burns had healed, the little bear was sent to live at the National Zoo in Washington, D.C.

MISTAKES IN AMERICA'S NATIONAL PARKS

As some of American's national parks were developed, starting with Yellowstone National Park in 1872, a policy concerning bears was also begun that has come to haunt today's park managers. Bears living in the parks' wildernesses began feeding on the garbage dumps established by park hotels. By the 1930s, feeding refuse to bears had become a daily institution, particularly in Yellowstone and Yosemite. Bleachers were erected at official feeding sites, and the bear shows, complete with ranger commentary, became favorite tourist attractions. The bears, used to seeing people in such proximity, lost their wariness toward them. Many learned to panhandle food from passing tourists. Mistaking these animals as "tame" bears, park visitors developed their own tradition of treating them as they would household pets. The sight of one of these "cute" animals standing and begging for some morsel held out to it must have added to the confusion. Inevitably, this kind of familiarity led to problems. (The first death caused by a park bear occurred in 1907 in Yellowstone when a tourist prodded a grizzly cub in a tree with his umbrella. Moments later, the mother charged and he was fatally mauled.)

Some park bears became aggressive nuisances, raiding picnic tables and tearing open tents and visitors' vehicles in their search for an easy meal. Though maulings and deaths remained rare, injuries caused by a swipe of a paw or a bear's frustrated bite when a crowd pressed close were too common. Responding to this danger, rangers posted "Do Not Feed the Bears" signs in highly visible locations. But the signs were, and still are, ignored by many of the visitors who see a black bear near the road.

The next step was to close the dumps. This decision was based on the belief that national parks should be returned to their natural ecological state and that it was "unnatural" for bears to congregate at the dumps. Probably the most famous controversy in the history of wildlife management was sparked by two well-known wildlife researchers, John and Frank Craighead, who conducted a pioneering study of the grizzly bears in Yellowstone. From 1959 to 1971, these two intrepid brothers studied as many as 900 grizzlies. They urged the Park Service to phase out the dumps slowly to allow the bears time to adjust to

America's symbol of forest fire prevention, Smokey the Bear is one of this country's longest running and most successful advertising campaigns. (Used with permission of the USDA Forest Service)

ONLY YOU

Ringed by a curious crowd, an American black bear wanders through a campground in Tennessee's Great Smokies National Park. Nearly 80 percent of bear injuries are the result of careless attitudes toward black bears.

natural food sources. But the Park Service made the decision to close the dumps "cold turkey," and after a bitter argument, the Craigheads' research was terminated.

Since dump closure, bears have had to find new sources of food, which can be scarce. Hundreds of bears have starved to death, or were shot while exploring areas outside the park. The irony here is that in 1972, a year after the dumps were closed, the first fatal bear mauling in thirty years occurred. Since then, nearly a dozen more people have been killed by grizzlies in Yellowstone and Glacier National parks. With the incidence of bear attacks on the rise, there is talk again of creating new artificial feeding sites or "eco-centers." Researchers now agree that the ingestion of garbage is consistent with a bear's foraging strategy of maximum intake of high-quality food. This new proposal would feed the bears by killing excess elk and deer and hauling them by air to dumps in the backcountry, thus luring bears away from areas of human use. It is doubtful, however, that the wildlife-loving public would ever let the Park Service go through with the idea.

With black bears, it's another story. Black bears in parks exhibit remarkable cunning and restraint in getting food from people. They are first-class actors, too, when it comes to panhandling. I once spent two weeks watching people and bears interact in Tennessee's Great Smokies National Park. Every evening at the Pinnacles Picnic Area, several bears would come out of the forest and make their rounds, investigating every picnic table. At first people would gather up their dinners and climb into their cars until the bears had passed. I remember one woman who leaped into her car with only the spatula she was using to turn the hamburgers. The bear got the burgers, potato chips, and buns. Eventually, a few people would start tossing sandwiches and other tidbits to the bears. A crowd soon gathered and the bears would put on a show of begging antics. One day, a crowd of more than 200 people followed a bear for an hour. During that time, a woman set her eighteen-month-old child down next to a bear that had filched a watermelon from a nearby table. Stepping back, she photographed the two together. As the crowd of onlookers swelled, the bear must have begun to feel trapped because he made several bluff charges, scattering the other would-be photographers.

I was amazed at the restraint these bears displayed around people. One day I watched a man refuse to move when a bear came up to his picnic table. The bear began eating his picnic lunch, then stopped and looked up at the man, who was grinning over him. The bear suddenly swatted the man off the table, knocking him to the ground several feet away. I yelled at the bear and threw a handful of road gravel at him, driving him off. Running up to the man, I asked if he had been hurt. He wasn't, but he was embarrassed for the fool he had been. There wasn't as much as a scratch where the bear had hit him on the shoulder. Unable to retract its dangerous claws, the bear had hit the man with the heel of his paw.

When I related the incident to park rangers, they told me that shortly before I arrived to do my study, a man had tried to put his seven-year-old son on this same bear's back in order to take a photograph. The bear stood up, shaking off the kid, looked the man right in the eye, and slapped his face, again with only the heel of its paw.

These kinds of incidents are not condoned by park officials, but because of limited manpower and the overwhelming number of yearly visitors to parks (Great Smokies National Park receives nearly 10 million annually), it is simply impossible to stop them. Bears that become serious nuisances or have injured someone are removed. "We try to keep the females because of their reproductive potential, unless they are three or four-time offenders," says Bill Cook, resource manager for the park. "When a bear leaves here it goes to a bear sanctuary or other wildlife management area in another part of the state."

OTHER KINDS OF BEAR MANAGEMENT

By and large, the wildlife of North America is a resource managed by government for the public's benefit. Outside of the national parks, it is the state and provincial wildlife agencies that carry most of the burden of overseeing each region's bear population. Their duties include maintenance of adequate population sizes, implementation of hunting seasons and bag limits, and elimination of nuisance bears. Most of these institutions have biologists who help collect and analyze field data in order to monitor the agency's programs or recommend changes in them.

Bear hunting is still a popular sport all over North America. Each year, thousands of black bears and several hundred brown bears are "harvested" by licensed hunters. Without state-managed hunting programs, bears would have long ago been eliminated in many areas. But sometimes even a well-intentioned program can get out of hand. In Pennsylvania, for example, game managers, delighted by a steady rise in their black bear population, decided to create a special bear-hunting season. Bear-biologist Gary Alt explains what happened:

> In 1981 we established a one-day bear season. The number of licensed hunters suddenly jumped from ¼ million to 1 and ¼ million. In some places in the bear-hunting range, we found as many as 258 cars parked on less than two miles [3 km] of road. Some critics referred to it as a glorified Easter egg hunt. It was not safe for the hunters, let alone the bears, under those conditions, so we dropped back the number of hunters to 100,000 and conservatively started lengthening the season each year by a day at a time.

Problem bears are another big concern for local wildlife managers. As bear habitat is increasingly used by people, conflicts are unavoidable. Beekeepers, for example, often place their hives in areas frequented by bears. To the ever-hungry bear, a sweet-smelling beehive is just another meal. In an attempt to protect

Katmai National Park's excellent bear management policy allows visitors and brown bears to be able to fish peacefully in the same waters.

Top: Too close for comfort, an Alaskan brown bear and her cub wander along the beach near a pair of resting hikers. These bears are most likely habituated to human presence and will ignore the pair unless they are threatened by erratic behavior or learn to associate people with food.

Right: Larry Aumiller, longtime steward of Alaska's McNeil River State Game Sanctuary, displays a plaster cast made from the footprint of a very large brown bear.

their investments, beekeepers erect electric fences around their beeyards. Usually this defensive measure works, but if a beekeeper discovers his hives have been smashed, the result is often another dead bear. When I was a commercial bee-keeper, earning my way through college, we used electric fences. But we also deterred bears by urinating around the perimeter of the beeyard. This "scent marking" seemed to work; I was the only professional beekeeper in my district who never lost a hive to bears.

By far, the biggest factor in creating nuisance bears is human garbage dumped where bears can find it. Mismanaged municipal dumps are a good example. Garbage is becoming such an attraction to bears in Juneau, Alaska, that police are threatening people with fines of as much as $1,000 for putting trash outside their homes. Campers and hikers in the backcountry also turn bears into dangerous nuisances by improper handling of food and trash. Once bears learn to associate people with food, they are sure to become a problem.

RESEARCH ON BEARS CONTINUES

All across North America, the world's most active region for bear research, numerous programs are being conducted that will help increase our understanding of how bears can fit into our modern world. The U.S. National Park Service employs a nationwide computer network, the Bear Information Management System (BIMS), to make reports of bear-related events available to managers in parks and regional offices. The BIMS is also being used as a research tool to monitor bear population trends and to track long-term behavioral trends. "We have just completed coding the 16,000 sighting and encounter records currently in the system," says Katherine Kendall, research biologist in Montana's Glacier National Park. "We hope to shed light on how bear behavior has been modified over the years by visitor contact."

In a modified World War II POW prison, Dr. Charles Jonkel of the University of Montana in Missoula conducts an experiment that is popularly referred to as the "bear school." Called an "aversive conditioning laboratory" by Jonkel and his colleagues, the facility is intended to teach bears to give humans a wide berth. The therapy involves scaring the bear with certain devices until the bear no longer attempts to approach—or charge—people. "We have a whole bag of

Exhibiting its species' famous curiosity, a polar bear investigates a pickup truck near Churchill, Manitoba.

tricks," says Dr. Jonkel. "They include a bear 'thumper,' ultrasonic noise, shark repellent, rapidly inflating balloons and a spray of red pepper oil [Counter Assault]. The pepper spray has been the most effective." The idea is to condition the bear to associate people with an undesirable consequence. Each bear is put into a cage containing two cells: a big one with lots of space and water in it and a smaller, darkened sanctuary area. To administer the therapy, a researcher typically stamps on the floor in front of the big cell, provoking the bear to charge. The aggressive animal is then sprayed in the face with the stinging red-pepper spray, inducing it to quickly retreat into the sanctuary cell. After two or three of these sessions, the bear learns to run the other way whenever a researcher presents himself. Then the animal is ready to be released back into the wild. Of the thirty-plus bears that have been released so far, only two have ever gotten back into trouble.

Aversive conditioning is now being attempted on problem bears in the wild. If a bear has been harassing campers in Alaska's Denali National Park, two "bear technicians" are sent to the scene to try to correct the situation. According to John Dalle-Molle, resource manager for the huge park, the bear involved in the incident is immobilized with tranquilizers and fitted with a radio collar. At intervals throughout the summer the bear is located and a tent simulating a backpacker's camp is set up where the bear will notice it. If the bear approaches within 100 feet (30 m) of the camp, it is hit with a plastic slug. "We remain quiet inside the tent so the bear will hopefully associate the unpleasant experience with the camp rather than the people, since bears often raid camps at night or when hikers are away during the day," explains Dalle-Molle. The model, color, and number of tents used are varied to help give the bear the idea that all camps are to be avoided. Evidently, the strategy is working. "None of the bears we have hit with the slugs have appeared aggressive afterwards," Dalle-Molle says. They are much more wary when near a camp.

The Federal Aid in Wildlife Restoration Act, better known as the Pittman-Robertson Act after its principal sponsors, has financed a great deal of the bear research conducted in the United States since the measure was introduced in the 1930s. The act allows state conservation programs to be financed through funds gained from a 10 percent excise tax from the sale of firearms, ammunition, and archery supplies used in sports hunting. Since 1937, the Pittman-Robertson Act has provided some $1.5 billion for wildlife restoration. For black bears, the results have been dramatic. Once reduced to scattered, remnant populations in the eastern United States, they now exist in healthy numbers in at least thirty states. Much of the biological research necessary for their recovery was made possible by these funds.

Techniques for safely trapping and handling bears often have had to be developed from scratch. In the 1950s, for example, a graduate student at Michigan State University, named Al Erickson, began tagging black bears. First Erickson and his helpers wrestled a live-trapped bear to the ground with chains and chokers; then, sticking an ether cone over its snout, they did their best to hold on until it passed out. Capture and handling methods have greatly improved since then. Working in Yellowstone National Park, twin brothers Frank and John Craighead gained national attention for their work involving trapping, drugging, and radio-collaring grizzlies (brown bears). Today, thanks to their pioneering work and that of hundreds of other biologists, the field procedures for studying bears have been fairly well mapped out.

In open terrain, working from helicopters is often more efficient and safer than conducting ground-based operations. In this case, a specially modified shotgun fires an anesthetic filled dart at the bear. Tipped with a hypodermic needle, the dart injects the drug under the bear's skin upon impact. The primary

Top: A wildlife biologist shoots a live-trapped Montana grizzly with a dart containing a drug that will soon render the bear unconscious.

Left: The drugs begin to take effect almost immediately; in a few minutes the bear is peacefully asleep.

Right: Montana bear biologist Doug Wroe measures an anesthetized brown-color-phase black bear. The paper bag is placed over the head to protect the bear's eyes from sunlight, as the drugs cause the bear to loose its blinking response.

Below: Canadian wildlife biologist Bruce McClellan and his wife prepare to place a radio collar on an anesthetized grizzly.

With the bolts finally tightened, this radio collar will be able to provide information on the bear's movements for up to three years. Some collars are designed to fall off after being worn for a certain length of time.

drugs used for bear immobilization now-a-days are a combination of xylazine and ketamine hydrochloride. These two drugs replace most other agents, such as an earlier drug called M-99, which have proven themselves potentially dangerous to the bears. Scientists still accidentally kill bears with tranquilizer darts now and then, but 1 or 2 percent death rate is now considered high. (In any project in which the animals must be handled, the possibility of capture-related mortality cannot be eliminated.)

After the anesthetic takes effect, the bear becomes unconscious and totally relaxed; often the animal can be heard snoring. Because the bear loses its blinking response, the eyes are dabbed with ointment and covered with a cloth to keep them from drying out or being injured by bright sunlight. Then the biologist pulls a tiny premolar tooth that will be used to accurately determine the age of the bear. Using an odd-looking pair of pliers, a number is tatooed on the bear's lip to permanently mark the animal. After taking blood and hair samples, the researchers clip a plastic or metal tag to an ear and take body measurements. If the bear is caught again in future years, the data from the first capture will be compared with the new.

If the bear's movements are to be recorded, a radio collar is placed around its neck. Most radio collars are made from two layers of 5-ply industrial-grade riveted neoprene. The entire transmitter and its battery is placed inside an aluminum container and then sealed with waterproof resin. The short antenna runs between the layers of belting. A pulsing signal of a specific radio frequency allows the biologist to track the bear for as long as two years. The signal can carry in a straight line of sight for up to 25 or 30 miles (40 to 48 km). "But you never get a straight line of sight," says Canadian researcher Bruce McClellan. "Trees, bumps, hills, gullies—all these really affect the signal. If I can get a reading as far as 5 or 6 miles [8 to 10 km] away, then I feel we're doing good." Using a highly directional antenna, the biologist takes several "fixes" on the pulsing signal from different locations. Then the bear's position is plotted on a map by triangulation. Sometimes a radio-collared bear is tracked by an airplane equipped with a special antenna on each side of its fuselage. The radio operator switches back and forth between antennas to determine which one receives the stronger signal and then sends the pilot in that direction.

Recently, satellites have also been pressed into service to monitor radio-collared bears in the high arctic and in Montana. Thus a polar bear's signal can be plotted thousands of miles away. Researchers can even tell if the bear should happen to die, because many radio collars are now equipped with a motion-detecting circuit. When the animal remains absolutely still for a certain period, a "mortality circuit" is activated. Taken together, these radio-telemetry studies have revolutionized wildlife research by allowing scientists an intimate look at a species' home range size and its seasonal movements and dispersal patterns.

CONSERVING BEARS: A WORLD VIEW

The bears' future is inextricably linked to that of humans. What we, as a species, do to this planet affects all other life. Why, you might ask, should we concern ourselves with protecting animals that are potentially dangerous? Well, for one thing, the presence of bears is a good indicator that our remaining natural habitat is still healthy.

"Deforestation, for example, is a local, regional, and global threat, because it adversely alters habitat essential to bear survival," says Lance Olsen, president of the Great Bear Foundation. "But there's more here than meets the eye, not especially what happens to any particular mountainside, but because deforestation is becoming so extensive in so many regions of the world that it can be expected to alter the hydrological cycle." This is the cycle that brings fresh water to continents through moisture-laden ocean air masses. Normally, much of the water that falls as rain and snow is prevented by vegetation from quickly running back to the sea. Aquifers are recharged by water that penetrates the soil, and the air is moistened and cooled by evaporation and transpiration from plants. But when enough land has become deforested, the process is reversed. The rains become diminished and much of the water that does fall is lost by rapid runoff. The land becomes arid.

"We have considerable, reliable evidence in our files to support a hypothesis," continues Olsen,

> that not only regional, but global climate can change quite rapidly with sharply severe effects on most living species. I fully expect that at least some bear species will be strongly affected as a reduction in rainfall follows upon the heels of deforestation in certain regions of Earth.

Bears (like other large carnivores), because they are the top, or consuming end, of the food chain, are superb barometers of the planet's remaining resilience; cut down the trees, shut off the rain, dry out a region, and it's good-bye bears. But where there are still bears we can breathe a sigh of relief that at least that patch of the planet is still alive and well. How far gone is Earth? That question can be answered by the answer to another question—How far gone are bears?

Fortunately, over much of the world's North Temperate Zone, bears are still doing fairly well, by and large. Much of this success stems from attempts to conserve bears and bear habitats. There are problem areas, to be sure, especially where forestry and land-use practices have gotten out of hand, but taken as a whole, these parts of our planet have not yet lost their biological resilience. But this is not so in Asia and in some tropical regions where the effects of overpopulation and deforestation are taking a dramatic toll. Large areas are turning into barren deserts, resulting in loss of wildlife and impending famine for the human inhabitants who remain.

Only reforestation can push back the desert. For example, China's soil has borne the burden of 5,000 years of civilization—but just barely. Great regions have been denuded of forests, and the desert has reached out to take their place. In some of China's mountain regions, the annual recorded rainfall has been cut in half just since 1967, and average wind speed has increased from about 6 miles per hour (10 kmph) to more than 37 miles per hour (60 kmph). Now, in a concerted effort, China is moving to reclaim these lost lands and improve the climate by planting a massive shelterbelt forest that will be 4,300 miles long and 200 miles wide (7,000 by 320 km) when complete. Running parallel to the Great Wall, this shelterbelt is slowly becoming one of the most impressive features of the Chinese landscape. When I paid a visit to a tiny portion of this giant endeavor, many of the trees I saw were still very small. But the project was proceeding with intense effort; workers were hand watering each tree. Someday, bears may even be able to roam here again.

But first China and practically all of the rest of Asia will have to change its attitude toward wildlife. In every large city there is a burgeoning black market for rare and endangered animal parts, including bears. According to Tom Milliken of the World Wildlife Fund, illegal killing and importation of bears has become an appalling problem because of the fantastic prices they fetch on the black market. Many of these animals are killed only for their gallbladders, which is believed to possess medicinal properties. "The value of Asiatic black bears in South Korea is tremendous," writes Milliken. "An animal shot in Gonju in 1982 sold for 16 million won ($18,500 US) through public tender at a government-sponsored auction. Since then the price of gallbladder has soared." An undried 180 gram (6.3 oz) gallbladder from an animal killed by a poacher in South Korea was sold for 46 million won ($55,000 US) at a public auction. The meat of the same animal sold for 1.53 million won ($1,830 US).

There is an ancient saying in Asia, attributed to Confucius: "I like fish and I like bear paws. If I can't have fish then I would rather have bear paws." Bear paws are usually prepared in soup and are very popular throughout the Orient. "The value of the paws increases greatly through the distribution process," Milliken says. "Japanese importers pay about $75 US per kilo for Chinese bear paws which are packaged in 10 or 20 kilo boxes." Importers then sell the paws to wholesalers for about $100 US apiece. Restaurants pay nearly $200 US for each bear paw, which is prepared and served as a meaty soup to diners with exotic tastes and well-padded wallets. One of Tokyo's better restaurants may charge as much as $850 US a plate.

These big bucks have caught the eye of American poachers. According to the *Los Angeles Times,* black-bear poachers work year round in northern California to meet the demand for bear gallbladders and other parts in the Oriental medicinal markets of Log Angeles and Asia. Undercover agents in California, Oregon, and Washington have arrested several smuggling rings. From Virginia to Alaska, a number of undercover antipoaching networks are in operation.

Law enforcement officers admit that the real solution the problem would be a drop in price for these products. Evidentally, this is just what is happening in Asia. Publicity surrounding an attempt to import fake bear gall into Korea has apparently lead to public skepticism regarding the quality of the commonly available bear gallbladder stock and consumption reportedly has dropped. Some dealers have complained that the effect could lead to the closing of some of the thousands of clinics that specialize in bear gallbladder treatments. The Chinese are also making inroads in the black market by introducing "farmed" bear gall to the traditional medicine trade. On six bear farms near Harbin, in Heilonjiang Province south of Mongolia, cage-reared Asian black and brown bears are "milked" of their gall via tubes inserted into the gallbladders. These periodical "milkings" do no seem to hurt the bears and are much preferable to killing dwindling wild stocks.

Far left: One of the many booths in a Chinese medicine market displays bear skeletons and other rare animal parts for sale. Medicinal and "cultural" use of wildlife is a serious threat to the endangered animals of southeast Asia.

A keeper tends part of his stock of brown bears at the Noboribetsu bear farm on Japan's Hokkaido island.

Another conservation problem is the danger of depletion or even extinction of endangered wildlife populations by rich big-game hunters who pay a premium price just to shoot rare animals. Unfortunately, many countries are right in there with the program. For example, the Chinese Mongolians offer a $50,000 US round-trip, package-deal bear hunt, with an additional $1,200 fee if the hunter wishes to keep the trophy. A Peruvian safari to hunt the endangered spectacled bear can be arranged for $25,000 US. One hunter Mark and I know of has made it his life's ambition to shoot every variety of bear for his trophy room. This kind of hunting may be good for foreign trade, but the loss to our planet's wildlife heritage is incalculable. If concerned people cannot stop these practices, maybe they can influence the rest of the world to at least manage and conserve bears as a valuable hunting and wildlife resource. This is essentially what we have done in the United States.

Once a decision to manage the bear resource is made, much can be done to enhance their habitat. In certain parts of North America, logging operations are being conducted with bears in mind. Forest managers in British Columbia, for example, are leaving large buffers of timber as visual screens between the highly accessible roaded areas and the areas used by bears. In other parts of Canada and the United States, access roads are simply closed after logging operations are completed. This action checks recreation and hunting, both activities that can bring people into conflict with bears and other wildlife. In some areas where bears have been exterminated but the habitat has remained viable, biologists are learning to reintroduce animals transplanted from other regions. We cannot force the world to save its bears, but perhaps example and encouragement can bring us closer to that goal.

Raised in captivity, two brown bear cubs are put through their paces during training for a circus act at the Noboribetsu bear farm. Trained bears are a valuable commodity.

WARNING

GRIZZLY FREQUENTING AREA
TRAVERSED BY THIS TRAIL

BE ALERT

REMOVAL OF THIS SIGN IS ILLEGAL AND MAY RESULT IN INJURY TO OTHERS

☆GPO 776-681 11/83

SAFETY IN BEAR COUNTRY:

Some Do's and Don'ts

S ince bears and people are having to share more and more of the same habitat, this section is devoted to a discussion of personal safety in bear country. Most of the information was distilled from both peoples' experience and research with North American bear species, particularly this continent's most feared wild animal, the grizzly bear. However, much of this information is also applicable to other bear species around the world.

AVOIDING TROUBLE

Unfortunately, there is no simple formula or action that will protect a person in all situations involving bears. Bears are highly intelligent and individualistic and are capable of nearly as many responses in a given circumstance as a human. But there are some general guidelines that the average person can follow that will greatly decrease the risk of injury while living, working, or recreating in bear country. Hiking in the backcountry is certainly safer than driving to your corner drugstore. The Alaska Department of Fish and Game estimates the probability of being injured by a bear is about $\frac{1}{50}$th that of being hurt in an automobile accident in that state.

The danger posed by "wild" bears has been greatly exaggerated in the public's mind. Inexperienced people, intimidated by gruesome bear tales, may panic at just the sight of a bear, no matter how far away. A person carrying such a strong fear projects an "emotional aura" that can actually stimulate trouble. In fact, bears usually just want to be left alone. In most situations, they will even go out of their way to avoid encounters with human beings.

A graphic warning sign in Montana's Glacier National Park leaves no doubt of what could be encountered on the trail ahead.

A bear concealed in a bush is extremely dangerous when encountered at close quarters.

"It's interesting how often bears don't like to be seen," says Kathleen Jope, bear-resource specialist for the National Park Service.

> If you come into a meadow, for example, and you see a bear that isn't aware of your presence and you would like it to be, don't yell at the bear right then. Go back into the woods where it can't see you, then yell, let it respond (usually by running away) and then go back out into the meadow. It's best to let it respond before it feels it's been seen.

A major exception, and I cannot stress this point enough, is the bear that has learned to seek out human foods. Add to the equation a species like the black bear, which is considered benign in the public's eye, and you have a formula for trouble. In the Great Smokies National Park, I asked over 200 visitors why they had approached panhandling black bears so closely. Almost invariably, their attitude was that these were "just" black bears. A quick glance at some bear-attack statistics will show, however, that black bears are responsible for more than 80 percent of all injuries and property damage caused by bears on this continent.

According to Dr. Charles Jonkel, one of America's leading experts on bears, there is a kind of sliding scale of interaction that bears are pushed along on their way to becoming a general danger to humans. The first step in this process is called the "habituated" bear. "This means they won't run—they'll stand their ground and let themselves be seen," explains Dr. Jonkel. "These bears will go on about their business, not caring if you are there or not." But occasionally a habituated bear will attack someone, like a photographer, who presses in too closely. During the three years that Mark Newman and I worked on this book, at least four amateur wildlife photographers were killed by grizzlies in the United

States. Grizzlies, especially those with cubs, do not like being closely followed. Ordinarily, a habituated grizzly might begin to feel crowded at 60 yards (55 m). A mother with cubs, on the other hand, will often respond to the presence of a human who is still more than 150 yards (137 m) away. Almost every person I have seen attempting to photograph bears approaches so close that the bear's personal space is obviously violated. I strongly recommend using at least a 400mm or longer focal length telephoto lens or, better yet, go to a zoo if you want close-up pictures. Following a bear too closely can also create a "setup" that causes the bear to react aggressively to the next person it encounters.

The "conditioned bear" is the next step toward trouble on Dr. Jonkel's scale. These are bears that have made the association between people and food; they may approach people for handouts, eventually becoming nuisances. As these bears become more aggressive (the third step in the scale), they may even try to force food away from people by raiding picnic areas or confronting hunters at their kills. In some areas of the North, a few bears have learned that their bluff charges can cause a backpacker to throw down his pack to better climb a tree for safety. That pack full of trail food is really what the bear wants, so withholding the pack might frustrate the bear into an actual attack. Giving up the food may save the situation, but it only reinforces this aggressive behavior. It's a dilemma usually resolved only by the death of the bear.

Bears do not like to be surprised at close range and may attack during such an encounter. There are many things you can do to reduce your chances of meeting a bear in the wild, though. First of all, be alert and aware of your surroundings. Watch for bear signs such as fresh tracks, large scats, animal carcasses, torn-up stumps, or claw marks on trees. Traveling in a group considerably reduces any risk of encounter, because groups of people tend to make a lot of noise, warning any bears in the area. (No grizzly attack has ever been reported on a group of six or more people.) If traveling alone, you can make noise by calling out "Hey bear!" every so often or by rattling a can of rocks. The sweet tinkle of a bear bell tied to your shoelace can often serve as a nice warning of your approach. A study by Kathleen Jope in Glacier National Park has shown

A man scavenging at a municipal dump in northern Canada ignores a nearby bear. Records show that few bear incidents occur at dump sites. However, problems often occur when bears range out from the dump into residential neighborhoods during their search for more human food.

that bear bells are significant deterrents to bear attacks. Once they have learned to associate the sound of the bells with people, most bears take off for other parts of their territory. My only criticism of bear bells is that the ones currently being sold to hikers are really too small. The sound of a stream or even a breeze can easily drown them out. According to another study, in Glacier National Park, confrontations between grizzlies and hikers usually occur along trails at places with less than 100 feet (30 m) sight distance near outwash or meltwater creeks crossing the path. The reduced visibility and noise from the running water mask the approach of hikers. However, injuries per confrontation are highest off the trail. Apparently, grizzlies living near heavily used trails have become used to seeing people and therefore are not as likely to respond with fear-induced aggression.

Another way to make warning sounds is to carry a portable air horn like the ones used on boats. Letting out a periodic loud "honk" has been used with great success by some people. Whatever noisemaker you may choose, the idea is to announce your presence so that a bear has a chance to leave before you suddenly intrude unnoticed within its space.

Avoiding trouble with bears is largely a matter of good sense. Hiking with an unleashed dog for protection, for example, is a poor idea. A dog can easily arouse a bear to the point at which it will charge, and then 99 percent of the time that frightened dog will run straight back to its master. You could be in for a nasty time if an angry bear, hot on your mutt's heels, suddenly bumps into you on the trail.

In bear country, camp location and layout are very important for avoiding trouble. Do not camp along streams or lakes where bears are known to travel or if you have seen fresh bear signs in the area. In permanent camps, a few large tents or buildings are better than several small ones. Placing them in a line or semicircle (not scattered or in a circle) provides ready escape routes for any inquisitive bears and helps keep them from feeling confused or trapped by unfamiliar structures. Backpackers are advised to sleep in a tent rather than out under the stars. Place the open end of your tent close to a tree and sleep with your head toward the opening. Your sleeping area should be located at least 160 feet (50 m) from all cooking, food storage, and latrine facilities. Also, try to locate your sleeping spot upwind (based on prevailing breezes) and uphill from where you cook. Try to avoid cooking greasy foods such as bacon, ham, or hamburger as much as possible. Greasy foods are especially attractive to bears (and they won't do your arteries much good either). Do not bury food scraps; all garbage should be thoroughly incinerated in a hot fire. A bear's sensitive nose can locate garbage buried even under 2 or 3 feet (.6 to .9 m) of soil. Cans that contained food should be burned to remove any trace of food before being packed out as trash.

Incidentally, women in the backcountry should avoid using perfumed cosmetics and should be especially cautious during menstruation, as these odors may attract bears. Menstruating women need not avoid traveling in bear country as long they use internal sanitary protection (i.e., tampons) and burn these materials completely after use.

Studies show that inadequate food storage is the major contributing factor in bear incidents around camps and campgrounds. Unfortunately, there are numerous misconceptions among campers about just what constitutes proper food storage. Storing food in the passenger section of a car or separate tent may seem like a safe measure but it really isn't. I've seen bears walk through tents as though they were made of paper, and a determined bear can easily peel your car doors off their hinges.

In most regions, a hanging food-cache is adequate protection. Simply en-

In southwestern Alaska, a brown bear keeps a wary eye on a group of hikers who are unaware they are being watched. Bears usually withdraw when people approach too close.

A trio of foraging brown bears ignore some photographers at Alaska's McNeil River Sanctuary. Wildlife photographers can upset a bear by pressing too close. At McNeil, only bears are allowed to do the approaching.

close the food in a cloth sack and suspend the bag on a rope strung between two trees at least 12 feet (4 m) off the ground. The trees should be far enough apart that a bear climbing one of them can't reach out and snag the hanging food bag. If there are no trees in the area, place the food in a cooler or airtight bag and bury it at least 650 feet (200 m) from camp. If this seems impractical or if you can't bury the food, at least get it out of camp. It's also a good idea to locate your food cache in a place visible from camp so you don't surprise some curious bear when you return to fetch your dinner ingredients. Incidentally, the clothes you wear while cooking will be saturated with food odors. If possible, store them overnight with the food. More than one person has been nipped through his greasy pants in the middle of the night.

In some national parks where bears have been pilfering campers' food for a long time, even suspending your food bag or backpack between two trees may not be enough of a safety measure. Bears have learned what the ropes mean and simply climb the trees and chew through them. The best way to protect food-stuffs from bears is to keep everything, including leftovers, in bear-proof containers. Hikers in Alaska's Denali National Park are now required to carry their food in small, bear-proof cylinders provided by the park service. Made of tough ABS plastic (the material sewer pipe is made from), these 8-inch-diameter, 1-foot-long (20 by 30 cm) cylinders are equipped with tightly locking lids. Although the bear-proof container program has been very successful in Denali, widespread use of the canisters is not likely until an inexpensive model can be made available to the general public. The National Park Service is presently looking for an interested company to mass-produce the canisters for under $15 (US), so they may soon be in outdoor-supply stores.

If you expect bears to come visiting your camp at night you can rig an alarm system so that the intruder at least announces his presence. One method I have used successfully is to run fishing line about 2.5 feet (.75 m) off the ground around the trees circling your tent, take up any slack, and place the reel near your head. The reel's whirring in the night will quickly wake you. Another simple warning method is to burn some tin cans in a hot fire to remove every trace of food and tie them on a string across the openings between trees. Place a few pebbles in each can so they will rattle when a bear bumps the line. Precaution is the best prevention.

In the Far North, arctic oil-field workers are occasionally attacked by polar bears. Polar bears rarely kill people, and in these incidents, they may not even have realized what they were attacking. In the spring, ringed seals—the polar bears' main food supply—begin to appear near the drilling sites. The seals are about the size of humans, and by the time an attacking bear has discovered just what it has subdued, it is too late for its victim. (Polar bears are not known to feed on human bodies.) In Alaska, off the North Slope, professional polar bear spotters are now hired to keep watch for approaching bears.

Bear Encounters: What to Do

There is no single piece of advice that will work in all encounters with bears. Since each situation is different, I strongly recommend gathering as much information on the subject as possible, so that you will have a full bag of tricks should you need it. It may not be possible to predict exactly how a bear will react to you in an encounter, but it will help a great deal if you stay calm and assess the situation. Above all, do not run away. This may trigger the bear's natural pursuit response, and a bear is much, much faster than you are. (Many bears can run 30 to 35 miles per hour (48 to 57 kmph)). Bears are naturally shy of people, so they will usually leave if given the opportunity. If you see a bear at a distance, go back or make a wide detour around it. If you can't make a detour, at least wait until the bear moves away from your route. And if you can't leave the area undetected, let the bear first sense you by smell, if at all possible, by quietly moving upwind of it.

Sometimes a face-to-face confrontation is impossible to avoid. There seem

Unaware that this "park" bear is about to attack, a would-be photographer approaches an American black bear much too closely. By bending over to take the photo, he has lowered his body posture, initiating a charge. Although the bear made bodily contact, there were no injuries.

to be two major types of potentially dangerous close-range encounters. The first is food related—the bear has been attracted by human food or garbage and may aggressively try to obtain it. The other is the surprise encounter—you have suddenly come upon a bear at close range. In this situation, the bear may either run away or rush you, depending upon how it perceives the threat. Douglas Chadwick, in his 1986 *National Geographic* article, "Grizz: Of Men and the Great Bear," succinctly describes his sudden meeting with a grizzly:

> Few encounters with grizzlies are planned. They're sudden—like the time when I was just below the spine of a ridge among fallen rock slabs. Gnarled firs, barely waist tall, gave off the sweet sharp smell of the high country. The bear stepped out from behind a boulder. It had a ring of pale fur circling its chest and muscle-humped shoulders. I shrank back; it caught my movement. I stood exposed. The beast surged toward me and reared up to work over my scent with a head twice the size of mine. And it stripped away every illusion that separated me from nature. Then it left, as grizzlies most always do.

When confronting a bear, do not scream or wave your arms, as these actions will only provoke it. Do not make any sudden movements or imitate any of the bear's aggressive sounds or postures. Sometimes an aggressive bear will turn sideways to display its size while walking stiff legged. According to Dr. Jonkel, it may also stand broadside with its head down near or across its front leg, to signal that it wants no trouble if you don't. In any case, try to avoid direct eye contact with the animal. Staring can be interpreted as an aggressive signal. Remember, bears often treat people as if they were other bears. Threat displays are part of a bear's normal reaction to an encounter with another bear. These displays usually establish dominance without the need to fight. Unfortunately, it is hard to know just where you fit in the bear's social system. Your status may depend on many factors, including your sex, how big you are, the number of people with you, and the individual bear's own sex, age, size, and social status. Also, each species has a different temperament that influences the bear's reaction to you. Black bears typically use their forest habitat for protection. If cover is available, they will usually flee from humans. Most brown bears (grizzlies) will avoid contact with people if they can detect them in time, but if threatened or surprised, they can be extremely dangerous. The predatory habits and open habitat of the polar bear seem to contribute to this species' boldness toward humans. Sloth bears, on the other hand, are shy creatures and seem to panic when surprised.

If the bear you have encountered is very close, back away slowly, talking as calmly as possible, toward safety—your car, a building, a tree, or a large rock. If the bear keeps pressing you, drop some item, a pack or other article, to distract its attention. Bears have been known to vent their aggression on the dropped item, allowing time for the person to escape. *Drop food only as a last resort.* Avoid sudden movements and try not to show fear.

A bear rearing up on its hind legs is probably taking a careful look. North American bears do not attack in this position. However, if the bear begins "woofing" or champing its teeth, the animal is signaling that it has become very nervous or aggravated. Threatening bears do not curl their lips or show their teeth, as dogs do, but they may growl or even roar. These behaviors are good indications that the situation has become far more dangerous than if the bear were simply holding its ground. An agitated bear about to charge will lay its ears back. When that happens—watch out!

A bear charges at high speed, often crouched low to the ground, on all four feet. A charge may be only a bluff, where the bear veers to the side or stops short of the person at the last second, or it may be the real thing. Unfortunately, there is often no way of knowing for certain until the action is over. A bear continually assesses the cost/benefit of its actions, even during a charge. If it perceives you as a great enough threat, the charge may be carried through into an attack. If you are unarmed, your options at this point are very limited. If the bear is a brown bear, at the moment when contact is actually made (and only then), try to protect your head, neck, and stomach by lying on the ground on your side, curled into a ball, with your legs drawn up to your chest, your hands clasped behind your neck, and your head buried between your knees. Keep your legs tightly together and try to stay in this position even if moved. As difficult as it may seem, playing "dead" may be your best route to survival. Grizzlies often will abruptly cease their attack as soon as you stop struggling and no longer represent a threat. After leaving, the bear may retire a few yards away and watch you for a while. Look around very cautiously and be sure the bear is gone before trying to get up. The attack may be renewed and intensified if the bear sees you move.

Do not play dead if you are being attacked by an American black bear, however. In some cases black bears have been known to attack people with the intention of eating them. Playing dead just makes it easier for them to use you for a meal. Bear-attack expert Dr. Stephen Herrero, of the University of Calgary, Alberta, Canada, suggests that when it comes to black bears (except for those with cubs) the best defense might be a good offense. "Heavy objects such as axes, stout pieces of wood, or rocks are possible weapons," he says. "They can be used to hit a bear on the head, with the hope of stunning it and causing it to leave. Other aggressive actions by a person might include kicking, hitting with a fist, yelling or shouting at the bear, or banging objects, such as pots, together in front of a bear's face." In short, act aggressively and make it as difficult as possible for the black bear to subdue you. There are several recorded incidents of people successfully fighting and killing a black bear, armed with only a pocket knife or a large rock to bash in the skull.

Predatory behavior is different from threat behavior. A hunting bear does not bother with threat displays and will show no fear, but rather intense interest. It may make a fast direct approach or circle carefully before the attack. "People who run away, unless they have somewhere [nearby] to go, or people who act passively or play dead," Dr. Herrero cautions, "are simply inviting the black bear to continue the attack." However, fighting back is not a good idea in all cases. Black bears with cubs usually bluff charge and then retreat. Acting aggressively toward a mother black bear may trigger a protective attack. I would treat her with the same respect afforded a brown bear.

Bear attacks are usually over in a few seconds, but it doesn't take long for a bear to do a lot of damage. Most likely, the victim's worst wounds will be to the head, neck, and upper chest. If it is true that bears treat people as if they were other bears, then the placement of these injuries makes a great deal of sense. "Watch brown bears fight," an Alaskan bear-biologist once told me, "and you'll notice it's always face to face, with the bears biting and pawing each other's head, ears, neck, and upper shoulders." Adult bears usually survive these rough encounters with little more than a few cuts and scratches. Unfortunately, people in the same situation are much more fragile.

Only a tiny fraction of bear encounters end in violence. Most often the reasons for the attack are clear, but in a few cases the attacks seem unaccountable, at least at first. Here's a good example.

During the warm stillness of a mid-June evening, a young Dutch visitor, Saskia Roggeveen, met a "rogue" bear in Denali National Park. Saskia, a slender

Brown bears often fight face to face, biting and pawing each other's heads, ears, necks, and upper shoulders. Injuries to humans by brown bears are frequently in these same body parts.

twenty-eight-year-old woman, and her companion, Darrell Tubbs, were walking from the Park railroad station to the collection of sleeping cars that makes up the youth hostel. The path follows about 200 yards of railroad track.

Something was crashing about in the woods on their side of the track. Fearing that it might be a bear, they crossed over the three sets of tracks to the other side. Then Saskia looked back. There was a large grizzly bear running out on the tracks. It stopped, let out a roar, and then charged. The bear was about 50 yards away. Saskia and Darrell scrambled down the railroad embankment, thinking that if they were out of its sight, they would be out of its mind as well. The plan didn't work.

Darrell was running just ahead of Saskia and didn't see her trip. The grizzly caught up to the woman and bit her, sinking its teeth into her buttocks and legs. As she screamed, Saskia had the impression the bear was looking for a good spot to grab, which it found when it reached her foot. Grunting and growling, the bear yanked and bit through the foot, mangling it. Saskia's screams turned to low moans. Terrified and not knowing what to do, Darrell just stood and watched. The grizzly bear was at least four times his own size. Then came the southbound train blowing its whistle. The bear took a quick look and lumbered off, leaving the injured woman behind. Her foot was saved only after a long night's operation in an emergency room.

It seemed amazing to nearly everyone that a grizzly would attack someone practically in the train station. However, a hard winter and a late spring evidently had driven some of Denali's wildlife into the lower elevations around the developed area near the park entrance. During the night before the attack, two moose calves had been killed by bears in the area. Later, during the day, rangers removed the carcasses. The attacking bear may have been angry about the loss of its food cache and was confronting Saskia and Darrell as the pilfering culprits. No matter what the reason, running away was the wrong thing to do.

PERSONAL PROTECTION AND BEAR DETERRENTS

Life-or-death situations with bears are really very rare; you have a greater chance of being struck by lightning. But it is still a good idea to be prepared. The most traditional piece of equipment a person can carry for protection against bears is a gun. Although thousands of bears are legally killed each hunting season throughout the United States and Canada, surprisingly few people who venture into wildlands have very much knowledge about guns. Even fewer know where to shoot a bear to kill it quickly. I am not very keen about having to kill bears, but I often carry a gun when I'm working in the field around them. Except when one is hunting for meat, shooting a bear should be done only as a last resort. After having talked to hundreds of campers and hunters, I feel that in the interest of safety, a discussion in this book about guns and shooting is appropriate.

In over sixty of the private interviews that I conducted during the summers

Two backpackers armed with shotguns carefully monitor an approaching brown bear. Surprise bear encounters may occur when the noise of a stream masks those of a hiker.

of 1985 and 1986, backcountry hikers in four U.S. national parks in Alaska, Washington, Montana, and Tennessee admitted to me that they were carrying a handgun for protection against bears. Although carrying firearms in national parks is illegal, almost everyone said that they would rather be fined for carrying a firearm than be mauled by a bear. I can understand their feelings, but most of these people were actually putting themselves at greater risk. Carrying a gun can create an air of overconfidence that can lead to trouble. Many of the guns carried by the people I talked to were stowed in backpacks or in such awkward places as to be almost impossible to reach in an emergency. Also, many of the guns were of too small a caliber to do much damage to a bear. The use of handguns for protection against bears is controversial at best. Besides, as Ben Moore or Alaska discovered, they don't always do the job quickly enough. This clip from the *Anchorage Daily News* tells his story of an encounter with a female grizzly near the town of Healy:

> "It seems like slow motion when it's happening. It got me by the leg first and shook me. Then it slung me about 6 or 8 feet [2 to 2.5m]. That's when I got off my second shot. I hit her in the side, I remember seeing the blood coming out. When she went for my head, I felt the pressure on my skull and heard the bones going 'crunch, crack.' I really thought I had had it." For some reason, Moore said, the bear released its grip for an instant and he fired again. "I wasn't going to give up. I still had the pistol in my hand. I put the muzzle in her mouth and pulled the trigger; she just shuddered." The bear slapped the gun away and ambled off. Moore said he was nearly blinded but struggled frantically to get the gun and reload it because he expected the bear to return. One of his eyelids was slashed and the eye protruded from the socket. Moore's nose was torn and shoved to one side of his face. "There was little pain, only anger," he said. "I wanted her to come back and finish the fight. But I'm glad she didn't." Moore said in the future he would carry at least a .44-caliber pistol, because the .357 Magnum, while eventually ending the attack, was not large enough to stop it quickly."

Ben Moore was very lucky. Although handguns are capable of killing an enraged bear, usually the human victim is killed first. Bears are just not that easily killed, even with rifles. There are many accounts of these animals being shot several times and then continuing to live on for years. One deer hunter in southeast Alaska, faced with a charging brown bear, is said to have fired 37 slugs into the animal with a .30-30 before he finally hit a vital area and killed it. (A bear's heart is very low in its chest and is rarely hit by hunters.) Many experienced Alaskan hunting guides commonly carry really big caliber (.375 H. and H. Magnum and .458 Winchester) rifles loaded with 300 grain bullets as backup guns for their clients' mistakes.

If you are confident with a rifle, a .30-06 or comparably powered weapon with open sights (no scopes) is suitable for protection against bears. But, because rifles require more accuracy in a high-pressure situation, many people (including most bear researchers) prefer shotguns. I carry a short-barreled, 12-gauge pump-action gun, with a modified choke, loaded alternately with rifled slugs and 00 buckshot. (Some field biologists use only slugs because they have more penetrating power than buckshot. Buckshot, however, does not have to be aimed as accurately in close quarters.) I usually load four rounds of ammunition in the gun's magazine. Sometimes I keep a blank cartridge or a "cracker shell" in the chamber to be used first as a warning shot. It can be quickly ejected if the attack is for real.

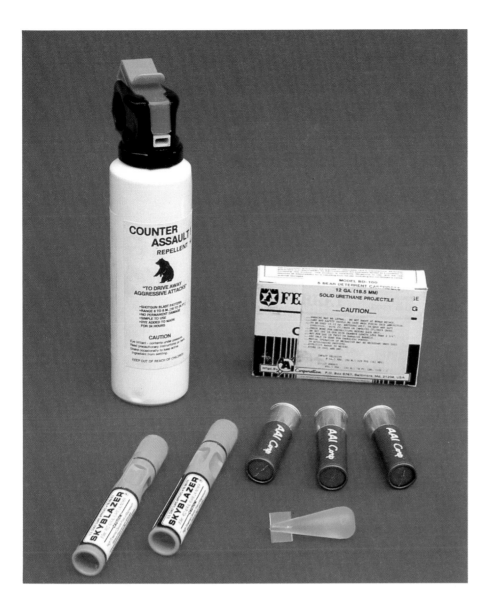

Some of the nonlethal deterrents that are now available for defense in bear encounters. The spray canister is becoming popular with hikers in national parks.

The decision to shoot a charging bear has to be made quickly. Canada's Northwest Territories Renewable Resources reference manual, "Safety in Bear Country," offers terse advice to anyone wanting to know when to shoot:

> The right moment for you to squeeze the trigger depends on your experience and confidence with a gun, how fast the bear is approaching, and your nerves. Everyone has a different threshold, or imaginary line, at which they shoot. Many experts recommend waiting until the bear is within 20 meters [66 feet] before shooting, others may feel confident waiting to see if the charge is a bluff. The decision can only be made by the person facing the bear. Remember, an accurate shot fired at close range has a greater chance of killing a bear than one fired from further away.
>
> The first shot is the most important, aim for the low neck if the bear is broadside, low center neck between the shoulders if the bear is facing you, or the front shoulder area in order to knock the bear down and disable it. Avoid head shots, as they often do not kill a bear. Do not stop to check the results of your shot. If the bear goes down, keep shooting vital areas until it is still. Make sure it is dead.
>
> If you injure a bear, it is your responsibility to find it and kill it. At least two armed and organized people are needed to track a bear. Stay together, keep guns ready and communicate. Be prepared for a close encounter with an angry bear.

The deterring effects of the red-pepper spray being tested here on a captive brown bear in Hokkaido are immediate.

A number of fatal maulings in Montana's Glacier National Park have prompted the construction of an experimental fenced enclosure designed to protect visitors camping in prime bear habitat.

After killing a bear, wait at least fifteen minutes before approaching the carcass. "Dead" bears have been known to come to life suddenly.

Carrying a gun is often distasteful or impractical to many backcountry users. In recent years, a number of nonlethal weapons for dealing with dangerous bears have been developed. Several of them show great promise. (At the end of this chapter, I have listed the names and addresses of several manufacturers and dealers.) Two of these weapons are nonlethal cartridges designed to be fired from a shotgun. One is a simple noisemaker, a firecracker fired at the bear. Originally designed for scaring birds in fruit orchards, these "cracker shells" are often very effective in deterring an overly curious animal. In Churchill, Manitoba, cracker shells are distributed free of charge by wildlife conservation officers in a public program aimed at deterring polar bears without killing them. Cracker shells can also be fired in modified starter pistols of the kind commonly used in athletic track meets. (Starter pistols are not legally considered to be firearms.) The other shell is a plastic projectile that is currently being tested in a scientific program to deter polar bears in the Hudson Bay area near Churchill. Fired at a bear's rump, the polyurethane projectile provides enough wallop to turn a bear and keep it running. In every instance during numerous trials, the plastic bullet has proven effective, even at ranges of over 100 feet (30 m). Once, when Mark Newman and a friend were photographing brown bears on Alaska's Kodiak Island, a bear came intimidatingly close. They fired one of these bullets at the bear's hindside, and the bear hurried away, never to return. By contrast, the kitchen of a fisherman's camp on the same island was also raided by two subadult bears that week. The scared campers, lacking a nonlethal deterrent method, shot and killed the two bears.

Another nonlethal personal weapon is a chemical-filled spray can with a quick-draw holster. Since it is not a firearm, it is acceptable for use inside U.S. national parks. The spray, marketed under the trade name "Counter Assault,"

A Canadian conservation officer sets a culvert live-trap in hopes of catching a black bear that has become a nuisance in a city park. Often the bears are "disposed of" after capture.

Stopping traffic, a grizzly casually crosses a wilderness road in Alaska's Denali National Park.

has an active ingredient consisting of 10 percent oleoresin capsicum (red pepper oil). It is nontoxic and has proved effective at stopping bear attacks during the few times it has been used in the field. I credit the spray for saving my life during an attack by a Asian black bear in Japan.

The night after the Asian bear attack, I received an invitation to go to Hokkaido to participate in a test of this spray on Japanese brown bears. In Japan, from two to six people are killed and from ten to twenty-five are injured by bears each year. (Guns are so strictly controlled that they are available to only a few individuals in Japan.) Using a captive bear, the entire test was videotaped for future study. The spray's effect on the bear was immediate, causing it to run to the far side of the compound. It sneezed numerous times and rubbed its eyes furiously in a effort to rid itself of the irritant. The chemical's major effects lasted for about five minutes and gradually wore off in about ten minutes. After seeing this, the Japanese researchers were as impressed as I was. They are very interested in making a product of this sort available to bamboo-shoot pickers and other forest workers who are at risk from bear attack.

OTHER POSSIBLE DETERRENTS

Numerous strategies to protect people and property from bears are constantly being developed and tested. Some have had no effect. Prior to our test of the Counter Assault spray on Hokkaido, for example, researchers there had tested a number of possible chemical deterrents, including pure hydrochloric acid. "The bears just licked their chops," one man told me. But the list of successful and practical deterrents is slowly growing: Solar-powered electric fences, for keeping bears out of established camp sites, seem to work fairly well, especially if the fence is well maintained. Some large construction camps in the Arctic are employing microwave motion-detection systems that operate by creating an invisible fence of microwave beams between a transmitter and a receiver. When an intruder passes between the two units, the beam is broken, triggering an alarm.

A very good and less high-tech early warning system is the use of several chained dogs in camp; it is important to use alert dogs that will bark when a bear approaches. To protect cabins from marauding bears some people lay ''nail boards'' in doorways and around building foundations. A nail board consists of a sheet of plywood with many nails driven through it. The exposed points of the nails serve as a spiked barrier to curious bears.

Although shouting humans can trigger a bear's aggression, in recent tests a loud radio effectively repelled polar bears. Radios seem particularly effective when they are tuned to a heavy-metal rock-and-roll station. Pencil flares of the type used on boats are another noisemaker that can be effective in turning a bear. Firing the flare creates a loud noise and sends a fireball of burning magnesium hurtling at the bear. It's enough to scare almost anything, but the one major drawback in using this kind of noise-deterrent is a very real possibility of starting an uncontrollable forest fire, especially in those areas where the woods are very dry.

SUPPLIERS OF NONLETHAL BEAR DETERRENTS

BIRD AND ANIMAL SCARE CARTRIDGES AND LAUNCHERS (Cracker Shells)
Margo Supplies Ltd.
Site 8, Box 2, R.R. 6
Calgary, Alberta T2M 4L5
CANADA

SCARE CARTRIDGES AND RACKET BOMBS
Marshall Hyde, Inc.
1344 Griswold
Port Huron, Michigan 48060
USA

12-GAUGE BEAR DETERRENT AMMUNITION (Plastic Projectile)
Attn: Law Enforcement Products
     A.A.I. Corporation
     P.O. Box 126
     Hunt Valley, MD
     USA 21030-0126   Telephone (301) 628-3782

(Note: The sale of these shells may be restricted. Inquire whether these restrictions apply to you or your organization.

COUNTER ASSAULT (Chemical Repellent Spray)
Bushwacker Backpack and Supply Company
Post Office Box 4721
Missoula, Montana 59806
USA

After reading practically everything published about bears in the past ten years, I particularly recommend the following works:

Bauer, Erwin A. *Bear in Their World*. Erwin A. Bauer. New York: Outdoor Life Books, 1985. In spite of the book's rather archaic title, it has a lively narration covering all three North American species.

Bears—Their Biology and Management. Papers of the Fourth International Conference on Bear Research and Management, 1977. This scientific volume is available through the U.S. Government Printing Office.

Craighead, Frank C. *Track of the Grizzly*. San Francisco: Sierra Club Books, 1979. The results of a pioneering research project in Yellowstone National Park.

East, Ben. *Bears*. New York: Outdoor Life Books, 1977. A bit dated, but visually appealing book discussing bears of North America with heavy emphasis on hunting. Written by retired editor of *Outdoor Life* magazine.

Flowers, Ralph. *The Education of a Bear Hunter*. Winchester Press, 1975. Autobiography of a professional bear hunter.

Ford, Barbara. *Black Bear: The Spirit of the Wilderness*. Boston: Houghton Mifflin, 1981. Good introduction to the North American black bear.

FURTHER READING

Herrero, Stephen. *Bear Attacks: Their Causes and Avoidance.* New York: Nick Lyons Press, 1985. A thorough study of the attacks made on people by North American grizzlies and black bears.

Kurten, Björn. *The Cave Bear Story.* New York: Columbia University Press, 1976. Explains the evolution of bears, with special emphasis on the cave bear.

Larson, Thor. *The World of the Polar Bear.* New York: The Hamlyn Publishing Group, 1978. An excellent, if dated, reference filled with photos of the Arctic and its bears.

McNamee, Thomas. *The Grizzly Bear.* New York: Knopf, 1984. Written as a month-by-month account of the bear's year, with asides on history and management and research.

Russell, Andy. *Grizzly Country.* New York: Knopf 1985. A many-sided view of the grizzly bear and the world in which it lives.

Schaller, George B. et al. *The Giant Pandas of Wolong.* Chicago: University of Chicago Press, 1985. A thorough and scientific study of the pandas in China's largest panda preserve.

Shepard, Paul and Barry Sanders. *The Sacred Paw.* New York: Viking Press, 1985. Discusses the bear in nature, myth, and literature.

INDEX

ADDITIONAL PHOTOGRAPHY

Dennis McAllister
Mel Douglas
Larry Thorngren
Jack Whitman